# First Crochet

# First Crochet

Lesley Stanfield

COLLINS & BROWN

First published in Great Britain in 2005
by Collins & Brown Limited
The Chrysalis Building
Bramley Road
London W10 6SP

9 8 7 6 5 4 3 2 1

British Library Cataloguing-in-Publication Data:
A catalogue record for this book
is available from the British Library.

ISBN 1-84340-278-5

Edited and designed by Collins & Brown Limited

EDITOR: Jane Ellis
DESIGNER: Penny Stock
PHOTOGRAPHER: Lucinda Symonds & Nicki Dowey
PATTERN CHECKER: Susan Horan

Reproduction by Classicscan Pte Limited Singapore
Printed and bound by Kyodo Printing Co Pte Limited Singapore

# Contents

How to use this book **6**

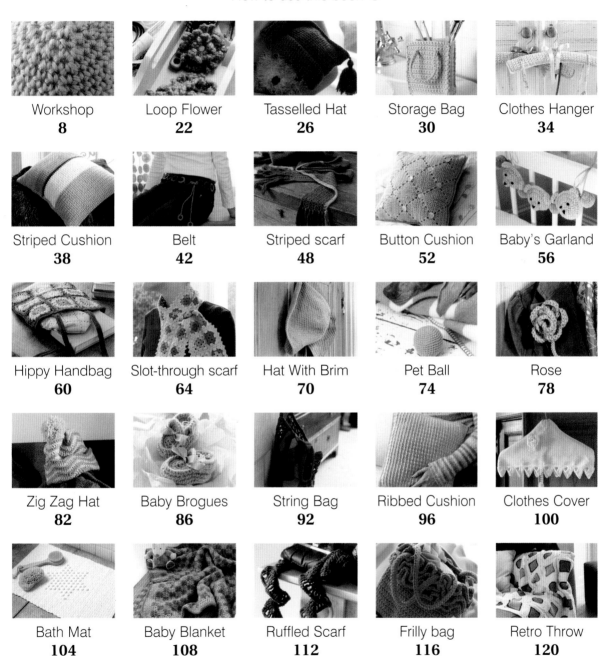

# How to use this book

If you have ever watched someone crochet and been fascinated by the darting movement of the hook and the speed with which the work grows you may want to try it for yourself. I know it's a cliché, but it's much easier than it looks! You only have to learn the language and a few simple techniques to be able to make some of the smaller items in this collection. All are designed with the beginner in mind and at the same time to be wantable gifts for yourself or others.

Don't be put off if your first attempts are mis-sized or mis-shapen. Just experiment with yarn and hook sizes until you feel relaxed and can make the right sort of fabric naturally and easily.

This book is divided into four chapters: Chain, Slip Stitch and Double Crochet; Treble; Shaping and Special Effects. The 24 projects are graded from extremely easy through to those which require a few more skills. They are all explained with instructions that follow the usual conventions, although abbreviations have been kept to a minimum. These row-by-row and round-by-round instructions are supplemented with pictures of the work in progress. The workshop illustrates the basics. If any additional help is needed the end flaps provide an instant reminder.

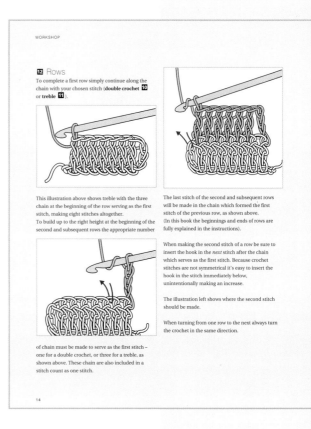

WORKSHOP

**12  Rows**
To complete a first row simply continue along the chain with your chosen stitch (**double crochet 10** or **treble 11** ).

This illustration above shows treble with the three chain at the beginning of the row serving as the first stitch, making eight stitches altogether.
To build up to the right height at the beginning of the second and subsequent rows the appropriate number

of chain must be made to serve as the first stitch – one for a double crochet, or three for a treble, as shown above. These chain are also included in a stitch count as one stitch.

The last stitch of the second and subsequent rows will be made in the chain which formed the first stitch of the previous row, as shown above. (In this book the beginnings and ends of rows are fully explained in the instructions).

When making the second stitch of a row be sure to insert the hook in the *next* stitch after the chain which serves as the first stitch. Because crochet stitches are not symmetrical it's easy to insert the hook in the stitch immediately below, unintentionally making an increase.

The illustration left shows where the second stitch should be made.

When turning from one row to the next always turn the crochet in the same direction.

14

A comprehensive workshop section at the beginning of the book features both diagrams and photographs, so you can see exactly what to do. Easy-to-follow text will teach you all the techniques you need to create the projects in the book. Each technique has a reference number, which is used for cross-referencing in the patterns and on the flaps.

### 13 Tension

Tension is the number of stitches and rows to a given measurement. It's essential that your crochet matches the tension given if the finished size is to be correct. Size isn't critical with many of the projects in this book but it's still a good idea to check your tension before you begin.

Make a tension sample several centimetres larger in each direction than the tension measurement. Insert pins to mark the number of stitches (and rows) given in the tension and then measure the

[...]et sample above shows how two [...]rochet form one ridge – you need to [...]when counting rows.

distance between the pins (see above). If the measurement doesn't match that in the instructions a larger or smaller hook should be used to achieve the correct result.

### 14 Rounds

Working in rounds means the crochet is all worked on the right side and isn't turned over, so a 'round' can even be square.

There are two methods of working rounds:
**1** After a chain ring has been made, chain makes the first stitch of the first round, then stitches

[...]e above shows the slightly [...]mation of [...]emphasize

The project section features 24 stylish items, starting with the very easiest and moving on to those requiring slightly more skill. Each one is accompanied by clear text and step-by-step photographs showing the key stages, for easy reference as you work. The instructions for each project contain reference numbers which direct you to the relevant technique in the Workshop, should you need to learn a new technique or be reminded of a familiar one.

---

## MAKING THE CUSHION

### Square
(make 18)

Make 5 **chain**. **6 slip stitch 7** into first ch to form a **ring 9**.

Working in **rounds 14** with right side facing.

ROUND 1  3 ch, 2 **treble 11** in ring, 3 ch. * 3 tr in ring, 3 ch;

rep from * twice, **ss 7** to top ch of 3 ch.
ROUND 2  3 ch,

1 tr in each of next 2 tr, (2 tr, 3 ch, 2 tr) in ch sp, * 1 tr in each of next 3 tr, (2 tr, 3 ch, 2 tr) in ch sp; rep from * twice, ss to top ch of 3 ch.
ROUND 3  3 ch, 1 tr in each of next 4 tr, (2 tr, 3 ch, 2 tr)

in ch sp. * 1 tr in each of next 7 tr, (2 tr, 3 ch, 2 tr) in ch sp; rep from * twice, 1 tr in each of next 2 tr, ss to top of 3 ch.
ROUND 4  3 ch, 1 tr in each of next 6 tr, (2 tr, 3 ch, 2 tr) in ch sp. * 1 tr in each of next 11 tr, (2 tr, 3 ch, 2 tr) in ch sp; rep from * twice, 1 tr in each of next 4 tr, ss to top of 3 ch.
**Fasten off 21** .

### Finishing

Set out two blocks of 9 squares each, the joins of each round facing in the same direction.

With right sides together, take 2 squares and **join with double crochet 22** : insert the hook under 2 strands of the first tr of 15 tr of front square and

under 2 strands of the corresponding tr of the back square, yarn round hook, and pull through a loop, yarn round hook again and pull it through 2 loops to make a dc.

Joining only the groups of 15 tr, join the remaining 7 squares of the back in the same way, then join the 9 squares of the front.

### Edging

Back: with right side facing, **join the yarn 20** at one corner and work

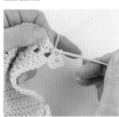

(3 ch, 1 tr, 3 ch, 2 tr) in corner sp. * 1 tr in each of next 15 tr, (2 tr in last sp of this motif, 1 ch, 2 tr in

of next motif, 1 tr in each of next 15 tr) twice, (2 tr, 3 ch, 2 tr) in corner sp; rep from * along each side, joining last side to first with ss in top ch of 3 ch. Edge the front to match.
**Fasten off 21** .

Press to shape.
Take the back and front and **join with dc 22** : wrong sides together and working through 2 strands of each pair of stitches, work (1 ch, 2 dc) in one corner sp. * 1 dc in each of next 19 tr, 1 dc in 1-ch sp; rep from * once, 1 dc in each of next 19 tr, 3 dc in corner sp. Continue in this way along 2 more sides, working 3 dc in corners, to the last side and work into the front only along this side to leave an opening for the cushion pad, ss to 1 ch.
**Fasten off 21** .

Sew a button to the centre of each square of the front.
Insert the cushion pad and stitch the opening closed.

# Workshop

Use this section of the book to learn the basics. Handling the yarn and hook will seem awkward at first but repetition will make the movements effortless and you'll quickly gain confidence and speed. Make a slip knot over and over again until you can almost do it with your eyes shut. Then practise the movement which takes the hook under the yarn from left to right, catching the yarn with the end of the hook and pulling it through the loop on the hook. When you have mastered this action you have all the expertise you need. Take the steps one at a time and don't go on to the next until you have really understood the structure of a stitch. Once you have graduated to treble you should be able to tackle almost anything.

# Getting started

Very few materials are necessary and you probably already have some items, such as a tape measure and small scissors. A round-pointed wool or tapestry needle is essential if you are not to split the yarn when sewing up.

Crochet hooks are of different weights as well as sizes, depending on the materials they're made from. It's as well to have a selection of sizes so that you can choose the hook that gives you the right fabric with the yarn you are using.

Choice of yarn is a most important factor and using the yarn specified for the project will eliminate some uncertainty. Otherwise, choose good quality, smooth but not slippery yarn, preferably in a natural fibre. Above all, be prepared to experiment.

## 1 Holding the hook

For most flexibility hold the hook like a pencil, then you can use your wrist as well as your fingers to manipulate it. You'll need to rotate it slightly, as well as push and pull. Holding the flattened portion gives the right balance. If the pencil grip isn't comfortable, try holding the hook overhand like a knife.

## 2 Holding the yarn

In the opposite hand the yarn should be threaded through your fingers so that it can be controlled evenly. This hand will also be holding the work as it progresses.

There are several ways to hold the yarn. My method is to simply take it over my first three fingers and under my little finger. Some people prefer to put more 'brake' on the yarn by taking it round the little finger, but everyone holds the second finger slightly

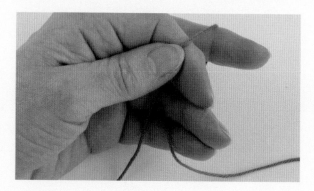

aloft. This is to hold the yarn fairly taut, ready for hooking.

You will have found the best method for you when the yarn is moving easily through your fingers.

### 3 Making a slip knot

You must first attach the yarn to the hook with a slip knot. My preferred method is this:

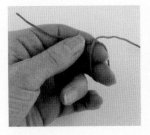

**1** Loop the yarn around two fingers.

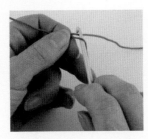

**2** Insert the hook in the loop and catch the long (working) end of the yarn.

**3** Pull the yarn through the loop.

**4** Hold both ends of the yarn and pull on the hook to tighten the knot.

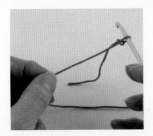

**5** Pull on the working end of the yarn to close the knot up to the hook.

### 4 Yarn round hook

This is the action used in all crochet stitches. The term implies wrapping the yarn around the hook, but in fact the yarn is held taut and the hook manipulated under and over the yarn to catch and then pull it.

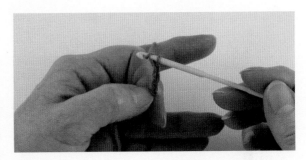

Holding the slip knot between thumb and index finger, with the yarn threaded between your fingers as shown in **holding the yarn 2**, flex your hook hand so that the shaft of the hook goes *under* the yarn from front to back – or left to right – and then *over* it to catch the yarn in the hook. Pull the hooked yarn through the loop already on the hook and you will have made a chain. Repeat this action to make a length of chain. This is explained in detail over the page.

### 5 Stitches

You now have the basic skills to make any crochet stitch.

All stitches start and finish with a loop on the hook. Crochet is always worked from left to right.

## 6 Chain

Chain is a loop or series of loops which can be used as the foundation of a piece of crochet, as the first stitch of a row or as part of a stitch pattern.

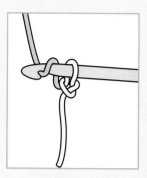

Having made a **slip knot** **3**, take the yarn round the **hook** **4**, then gently pull the yarn through the loop on the hook without tightening it too much. This makes one chain.

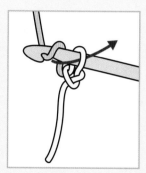
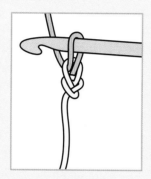

Repeating these actions makes a length of chain. The front of the chain is a series of V shapes (see below left), whereas the formation of the back is more difficult to distinguish. It's always the front that is worked into and the hook inserted under the top two of the three strands that make up a chain.

## 7 Slip stitch

Because it's simply a loop pulled through, in the same way as chain, a slip stitch has no height. It's usually used to join chain into a ring or as an invisible join in a stitch pattern.

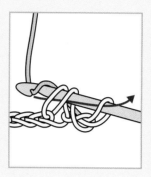

Insert the hook in the chain or stitch, taking it under the two top strands of the chain or stitch. Take the yarn round the hook (see left) and pull it through both the chain or stitch and the loop on the hook. One slip stitch has been made.

## 8 Making stitches

Always insert the hook in the top two strands of a chain or stitch unless the instructions state otherwise.

## 9 Chain ring

To join a length of chain into a ring with a slip stitch, insert the hook in the first chain, yarn round hook

then pull the yarn through both the chain and the loop on the hook. A chain ring makes a base for crochet worked in rounds, with the stitches of the first round made into the space in the centre, not into the chain itself.

## 10 Double crochet

This is a short stitch which makes a solid fabric when used alone and is a component of many stitch patterns.

**1** When working into a chain, miss one chain (unless instructed otherwise), insert the hook in the next chain, yarn round hook, pull the yarn through the chain to make two loops on the hook.

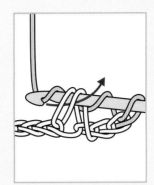

**2** Yarn round hook and pull the yarn through the chain to make three loops on the hook.

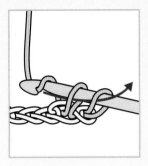

**2** Yarn round hook and pull the yarn through both loops on the hook.

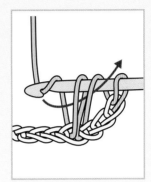

*(see step 2 image above)*

This completes a double crochet, which is the second stitch of the row, the first being the missed chain.

**3** Yarn round hook and pull the yarn through the first two loops on the hook.

**4** Yarn round hook and pull the yarn through the remaining two loops on the hook.

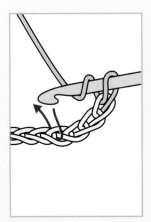

## 🔟 Treble

This is a taller stitch which is even more versatile for patterning than double crochet.

**1** When working into a chain, yarn round hook, miss three chain, insert the hook in the next chain.

This completes a treble, which is the second stitch of the row, the first being the three missed chain.

## 12 Rows

To complete a first row simply continue along the chain with your chosen stitch (**double crochet 10** or **treble 11**).

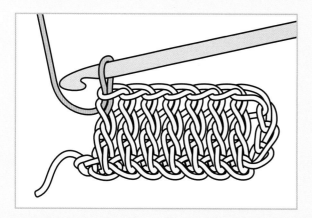

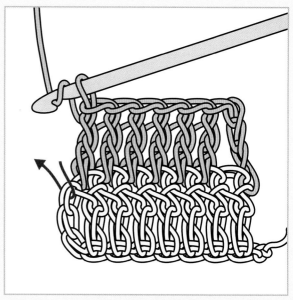

This illustration above shows treble with the three chain at the beginning of the row serving as the first stitch, making eight stitches altogether.

To build up to the right height at the beginning of the second and subsequent rows the appropriate number

The last stitch of the second and subsequent rows will be made in the chain which formed the first stitch of the previous row, as shown above.
(In this book the beginnings and ends of rows are fully explained in the instructions).

When making the second stitch of a row be sure to insert the hook in the *next* stitch after the chain which serves as the first stitch. Because crochet stitches are not symmetrical it's easy to insert the hook in the stitch immediately below, unintentionally making an increase.

The illustration left shows where the second stitch should be made.

When turning from one row to the next always turn the crochet in the same direction.

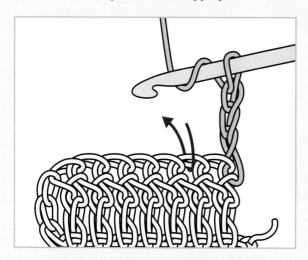

of chain must be made to serve as the first stitch – one for a double crochet, or three for a treble, as shown above. These chain are also included in a stitch count as one stitch.

The double crochet sample above shows how two rows of double crochet form one ridge – you need to be aware of this when counting rows.

The treble sample above shows the slightly asymmetrical formation of crochet stitches, emphasized by being worked in rows.

## 13 Tension

Tension is the number of stitches and rows to a given measurement. It's essential that your crochet matches the tension given if the finished size is to be correct. Size isn't critical with many of the projects in this book but it's still a good idea to check your tension before you begin.

Make a tension sample several centimetres larger in each direction than the tension measurement. Insert pins to mark the number of stitches (and rows) given in the tension and then measure the

distance between the pins (see above). If the measurement doesn't match that in the instructions a larger or smaller hook should be used to achieve the correct result.

## 14 Rounds

Working in rounds means the crochet is all worked on the right side and isn't turned over, so a 'round' can even be square.

There are two methods of working rounds:
**1** After a chain ring has been made, chain makes the first stitch of the first round, then stitches are made into the ring and the last stitch is joined to the chain with a slip stitch. In the same way, subsequent rounds are started with chain and

finished with a slip stitch (see the treble sample above).

**2** If there's no slip stitch at the end of the first round and no chain starting the next, the rounds will be

continuous with no sign of a join (as shown in the double crochet sample above) but there will be a 'step' at the end.

With continuous rounds, a marker will be needed to keep count of stitches and rounds.

## 15 Markers

The simplest way to mark rounds is to use a length of contrast yarn. Leaving the ends hanging, lay it from front to back or vice versa between the last

stitch of one round and the first stitch of the next. It will look like running stitch (see above). On completion, pull it out and discard it.

## 16 Slip ring

An alternative way to start crochet in the round is with a slip ring. This pulls up tight in the centre but is perhaps a little trickier than a chain ring for a beginner. Here it's shown as the basis of a round of treble.

**1** Make a loop as for a **slip knot 3**.

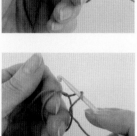

**2** Insert the hook in the loop and catch the working end of the yarn, as for a slip knot.

**3** Holding the ring closed with finger and thumb, make three chain.

**4** Inserting the hook under the two strands formed by the ring and the short end, make the required number of treble.

**5** Pull on the short end of the yarn to close the ring up before joining with a slip stitch to the top chain of the three chain.

## 17 Increasing

Increasing can be done at either the beginning or the end of a row. The principle is the same for both double crochet and treble.

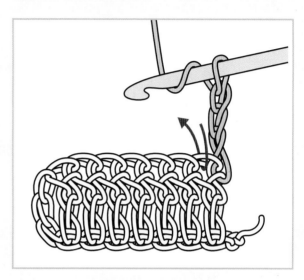

The first diagram above shows where the new stitch is made at the beginning of a row of treble.

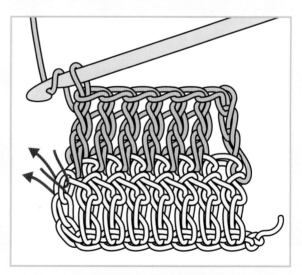

The second diagram shows where two stitches are made at the end of the row.

## 18  Decreasing

Decreasing a stitch is a little trickier as two stitches must be gathered together. This is done by working half a stitch into each of two adjacent stitches and then completing them as one.

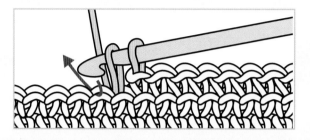

For example, to decrease one stitch in double crochet: * insert the hook in the next stitch, yarn round hook, pull the yarn through;

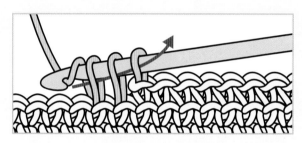

repeat from *, making three loops on the hook, yarn round hook, pull the yarn through all three loops.

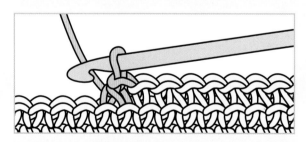

A treble decrease is worked on the same principle, but with the additional wraps and loops of that stitch.

## 19  Reading instructions

The language of crochet looks mystifying at first, but this is because abbreviations are used. By shortening the instructions they make it easier for you to find your place. You'll quickly learn that ch is chain, etc, and you'll have no difficulty following instructions.

Asterisks and brackets are there to help.

An asterisk (*) is simply a marker indicating a point from which a group of instructions is to be repeated. Square brackets also indicate a repeat – in this case, the number of repeats is stated after the brackets. Round brackets indicate a group of stitches to be worked together.

## 20  Joining new yarn

This is usually done at the beginning or end of a row but it can thicken a seam, so if the crochet is fairly close-textured it can be done mid-stitch and mid-row. Simply leave a short end of the first yarn then, leaving a short end of the new yarn, carry on. After a stitch or two you will be able to pull the two ends to close up any gap and then join them with a reef knot. After completion, undo the knot if it's bulky or leave it if it's not obtrusive, and 'darn in' the ends.

To join new yarn in a new place, for example when starting an edging, hold the yarn behind the work, insert the hook and pull a loop through, yarn round hook and pull it through the loop on the hook.

## 21 Fastening off

The loop of the last stitch is secured by breaking the yarn and using the hook to gently pull the end

through until the loop is lost. Leave a long end if it will be needed for sewing up.

## 22 Joining with double crochet

'Sewing up' with a hook instead of a needle is one of the most satisfying aspects of crochet. It's speedy and gives an immaculate finish.

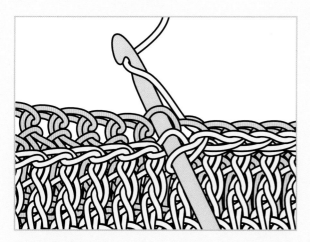

Hold the two pieces of crochet right sides together, insert the hook under the inside single strand of the first stitch of each edge, take the yarn round the hook and pull through a loop, yarn round hook and pull it through both loops on hook to make a **double**

crochet 10. Continue working double crochet in pairs of stitches in this way (see the diagram below left). If a firmer join is required the same method can be used, but inserting the hook under *both* strands of each stitch.

## 23 Finishing

Most of these projects will need light pressing to make sure they are the correct size and shape, and to give a smooth finish. Lay the item out right side down on a clean padded surface, such as an ironing board, and pin out to shape, with pins at every 2.5cm (1in) all around the edge. For pinning out or holding edges together use long quilting pins which won't get lost in the crochet. Make sure lines of stitches are straight and measure each piece to check it is the correct size. You can stretch or ease a piece to adjust it slightly. Press on the wrong side with a warm iron, using steam if it's advised on the yarn ball-band. Before joining motifs, square up squares and pin everything out to size and shape as described above. If you are working with lots of motifs of the same size, an god way of making sure they are identical is to draw a template with waterproof pen on a piece of plain fabric, and pin them out using this as a guide. Steam or press each motif with a damp cloth according to the instructions on the ball band, then leave to dry before joining together.

Large and open pieces of crochet may drop, but if you crochet seams together using the same yarn used for the project, as described in **joining with double crochet** 22, the seams will give in proportion to the rest of the work.

Lastly, darn in any ends.

## 24 Darning in ends

To darn in use a tapestry needle to weave each end invisibly into nearby stitches. End with a back stitch and snip off the end close to the crochet.

# 1

## Chain, slip stitch and double crochet

The six designs in this section require only the most minimal skills, so if you are a beginner you will need to practise first, but you should soon be able to make something. If you're unhappy with the way the project is turning out just unravel and start again. This sounds like brutal advice but it's better not to persevere hoping that a mistake will correct itself and then be disappointed. This way, you're learning and you're in control!

# Loop Flower

Make mop-head flowers for yourself or your friends. They can be used as decoration on a coat, a scarf, or as a hair scrunch.

Chain is usually a base for other stitches, but these flowers are made entirely with chain and slip stitches. A chain ring is filled with chain loops, then chain bars behind are filled with more chain loops.

## You will need

1 x 50g ball of Jaeger Matchmaker Merino Aran in pink
5.50mm hook

## Size
Approximately 6cm (2¼in) across

## Abbreviations
ch – chain; cm – centimetres; in – inches;
ss – slip stitch

# MAKING THE FLOWER

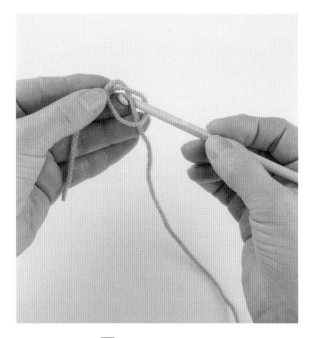

Make **slip knot** 3 .

Make 4 **chain** 6 .

**Slip stitch** 7 into the first ch to form a **chain ring** 9 .

ROUND 1 [10 ch, ss into ring] 8 times. 8 loops.

ROUND 2 [3 ch, take ch behind 2 loops and ss into ring] 4 times. 4 bars.

24

tip On round one work the slip stitches around the tail end of the yarn as well as the chain of the ring and you will then have one end less to darn in.

**ROUND 3** *Working behind loops, into next bar: ss, [10 ch, ss] 4 times; repeat from * 3 times. 4 loops worked in each bar.

**Fasten off 21 .**

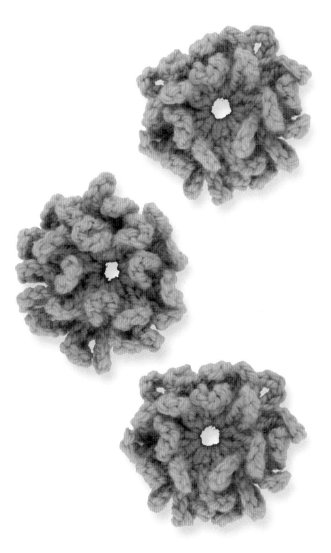

25

# Tasselled Hat

Swinging tassels are a fun addition to this simplest of all hats.

The hat is a continuous tube of double crochet which, instead of being stitched at the top, is joined with a row of double crochet. Simply add tassels.

## You will need

2 x 50g balls of Debbie Bliss Merino DK in orange
4.50mm hook

## Size
To fit age 3–6 months

## Tension
17 stitches and 20 rounds to 10cm (4in) over dc with 4.50mm hook

## Abbreviations
ch – chain; cm – centimetres; dc – double crochet;
in – inches

# MAKING THE HAT

Make 64 **chain** 6 . Without twisting ch,

**slip stitch** 7 into first ch to **form a ring** 9 .
63 stitches.

ROUND 1 Work 1 **double crochet** 10 in each ch.

With the right side facing,

continue to work in **rounds** 14 of dc for 19cm
(7½in).
**Fasten off** 21 but do not break yarn.
JOINING ROW **Join with double crochet** 22 . With the
right side still facing, yarn to the right and

holding the top edge closed: 1 ch, *insert hook under
both strands of next dc of front and corresponding

dc of back, yarn round hook and pull a loop through, yarn round hook again and pull it through 2 loops to make a dc in the usual way; repeat from * to end. Fasten off.

**Darn in ends 24.**

## Finishing

Fold back the brim.

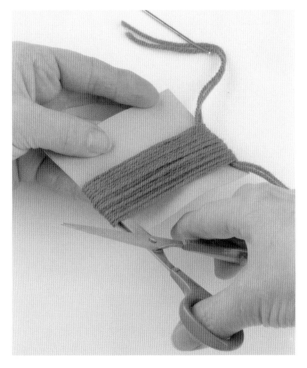

Use another strand of yarn to bind the tassel just below the top. Knot the doubled yarn at the head of the tassel and use this to stitch a tassel to each corner of the hat.

**Tassels**

Wind yarn around a 9cm (3½in) wide piece of card, enclosing a doubled strand at the top. Cut the yarn along the opposite edge.

# Storage Bag

A miniature tote bag makes a practical present in itself or it could be the container for a small gift.

Rows of double crochet make the rectangles that form the sides and base of the bag, while the handles are slip stitch worked into chain.

## You will need

1 x 100g ball of Sirdar Pure Cotton DK in turquoise
3.50mm hook
Wool needle

## Size

11 cm (4½in) high, 10cm (4in) wide, 7cm (2½in) deep

## Tension

8 sts and 10 rows to 5cm (2in) over double crochet with 3.50mm hook

## Abbreviations

ch – chain; cm – centimetres; dc – double crochet; in – inches; rep – repeat; st(s) – stitch(es)

# MAKING THE BAG

## Base

The bag is worked back and forth in **rows 12**.
Make 17 **chain 6**.

**ROW 1** Miss 2 ch, * 1 **double crochet 10** in next ch; rep from * to end, turn. 16 sts.

**ROW 2** 1 ch, [1 dc in next dc] 14 times,

1 dc in top ch of 2 ch, turn.

**ROW 3** 1 ch, [1 dc in next dc] 14 times, 1 dc in ch.

** Rep last row 9 times. Total 12 rows.

**Fasten off 21**.

## Back

As base to **.
Rep last row 19 times. Total 22 rows.
Fasten off.

## Front

As back.

## Sides

(make 2)
Make 12 chain.

**ROW 1** Miss 2 ch, * 1 dc in next ch; rep from * to end. 11 sts.

**ROW 2** 1 ch, [1 dc in next dc] 9 times, 1 dc in top ch of 2 ch.

**ROW 3** 1 ch, [1 dc in next dc] 9 times, 1 dc in ch.
Rep last row 19 times. Total 22 rows.
Fasten off.

## Handles

(make 2)
Make 48 chain.

Miss 1 **ch**, ***slip stitch 7** in next ch; rep from * to end.
Fasten off.

## Finishing

Wrong sides together and with stitches lying in the same direction,

use a wool needle to join a side to the back with stab stitch and an occasional back stitch, taking the needle under two strands of each stitch each time. Join the second side to the back in the same way and then join the sides to the front. Wrong sides together, join the base in the same way.

Use the crochet hook to pull the end of one handle from outside to inside between stitches on the back, then do the same with the other end. Knot both ends. Attach the second handle to the front in the same way.

tip   Remember that chain at the beginning of a row counts as the first stitch. So the 2 chain missed at the beginning of row 1 of the base of the bag comprise one stitch in the final count, as does the one chain made at the beginning of each following row.

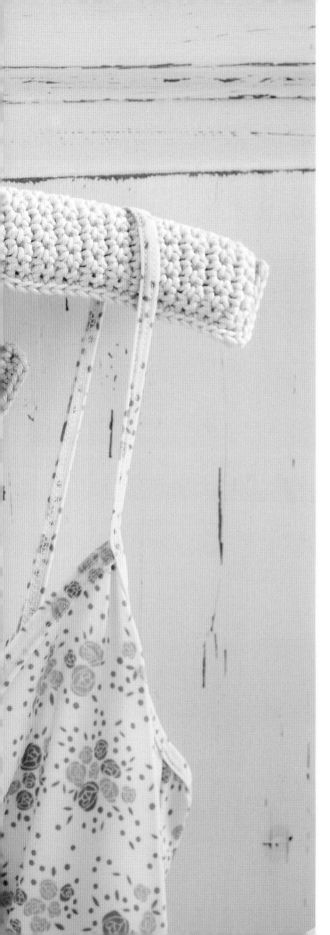

# Clothes Hanger

Transform a plain wooden coat hanger into a luxury item with few crochet skills and even less sewing know-how.

The cover of the hanger is a rectangle of double crochet, joined with double crochet on the right side for a neat, professional-looking finish.

## You will need

1 x 100g ball of Sirdar Pure Cotton DK in pale green
3.50mm hook
Wooden coat hanger
Lightweight wadding
Scissors, sewing thread and needle
Ribbon

## Tension

8 stitches and 10 rows to 5cm (2in) over dc with 3.50mm hook

## Abbreviations

ch – chain; cm – centimetres; dc – double crochet; in – inches

# COVERING THE HANGER

## The cover

Cut out a rectangle of wadding to fit over and along the coat hanger.

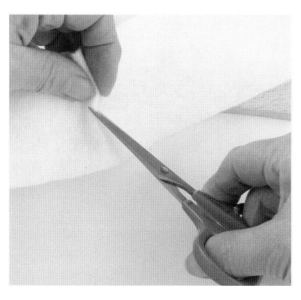

Fold the wadding in half lengthways, snip a small hole in the centre of the fold and push the hook of the hanger through.

Join the cut edges of the wadding by oversewing.

Make 15 **chain** **6** (or required odd number of ch to fit around padded hanger).

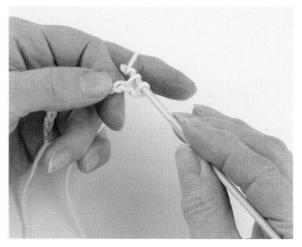

**ROW 1** Miss 2 ch, *1 **double crochet** **10** in next ch; repeat from * to end. 14 stitches (or an even number of stitches).

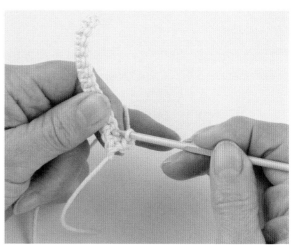

**ROW 2** 2 ch, *1 dc in next dc; repeat from *, ending 1 dc in top ch of 2 ch.
Repeat row 2 until the crochet is the length of the padded hanger and an even number of rows has been completed.
**Fasten off** **21** .

## Finishing

Fold the crochet in half lengthways and push the hook of the hanger through the centre.
**Join with double crochet 22 .** Starting at the fold, taking the hook under 2 strands of yarn each time,

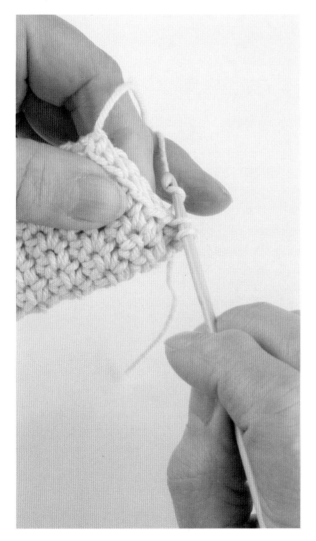

3 dc in corner, 1 dc in each pair of front and back row ends along the long edge, 3 dc in corner. Inserting the hook in the remaining single strand of each chain, complete second short edge as first.
Fasten off.
Trim with ribbon bow.

insert the hook in the first stitch of the front and corresponding stitch of the back, yarn round hook and pull through a loop, yarn round hook and pull it through 2 loops to make a dc. Work a dc in each pair of stitches,

# Striped Cushion

Colour is the key ingredient of this simple, stylish cushion with its cord-like edging.

The entire project, including the edging, is in double crochet. The last row of the edging is worked from left to right instead of right to left, which takes a little getting used to, but it isn't difficult.

## You will need

9 x 50g balls Debbie Bliss Cotton Double Knitting:

    5 balls taupe (A)
    2 balls ivory (B)
    1 ball chocolate (C)
    1 ball turquoise (D)

4.00mm hook
4.50mm hook
Cushion pad

## Size

30cm x 40cm (12in x 16in)

## Tension

14 sts and 17 rows to 10cm (4in) over dc with 4.50mm hook

## Abbreviations

ch – chain; cm – centimetres; dc – double crochet; in – inches; st(s) – stitch(es)

# MAKING THE CUSHION

## Back

With 4.50mm hook and A, make 43 **chain** **6** .

ROW 1 Miss 2 ch, * 1 **double crochet** **10** in next ch; rep from * to end.  42 sts.

ROW 2 1 ch, [1 dc in next dc] 40 times, 1 dc in top ch of 2 ch.

ROW 3 1 ch, [1 dc in next dc] 40 times, 1 dc in ch.

Rep last row 19 times.  Total 22 rows.

With B, work 14 rows.

With C, work 2 rows.

With D, work 8 rows.

With A, work 22 rows.

**Fasten off** **21** .

## Front

As back.

## Finishing

Matching stripes, place front on back, wrong sides together. With front facing, starting on a long side, using 4.00mm hook and A, **join with double crochet** **22**: insert hook under 2 strands of first st of front and under 2 strands of corresponding st of back, yarn round hook and pull through a loop, yarn round hook again and

pull it through 2 loops to make a dc.

Continue like this, working a dc in pairs of stitches and

working 3 dc in each corner, until 1 short side and 2 long sides have been joined.

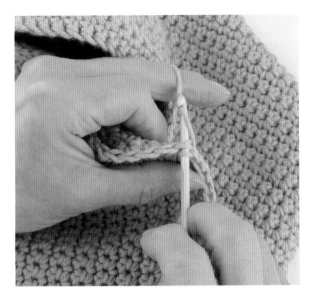

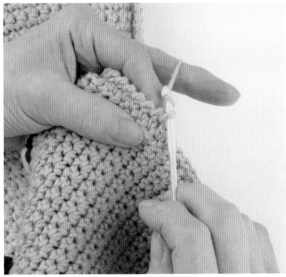

Along second short side work 1 dc in each st of front only to leave an opening for the cushion pad, join with a slip stitch to the first dc. Do not fasten off. With front still facing, work dc from left to right (sometimes called crab stitch).

Yarn round hook and pull it through 2 loops to complete dc. Work all stitches in this way. Fasten off.

Insert cushion pad and stitch opening closed.

Insert hook under 2 strands of next dc on right, yarn round hook, pull through a loop to make 2 loops on the hook.

# Belt

Crochet-covered rings can be made into a belt or even an entire garment if you feel experimental and want real 1960's nostalgia.

For a beginner, working around a solid object like a curtain ring can be a way to keep the stitches even.

## You will need

3 x 50g balls Jaeger Aqua:
    1 ball pink (A)
    1 ball purple (B)
    1 ball orange (C)
2.50mm hook
22 curtain rings, approximately 3cm (1in) diameter
2 smaller rings
Wool needle

## Size

83cm (33in) long, or required length, plus ties

## Tension

Dc to fit fairly closely around ring

## Abbreviations

ch – chain; cm – centimetres; dc – double crochet; in – inches

# MAKING THE BELT

## To make

Using yarn colour A,

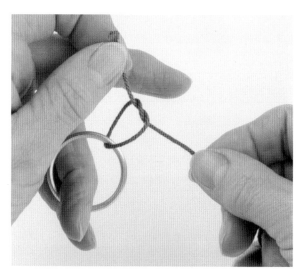

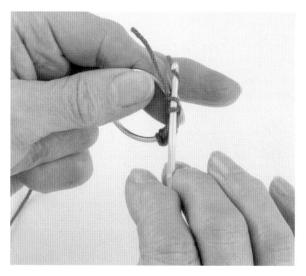

Repeat from * 31 times or until ring is filled with stitches.

make a single knot on one curtain ring (this replaces the usual slip knot).
Insert hook in ring, pull loop through,

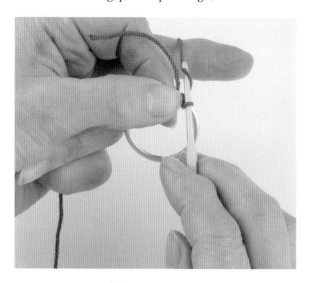

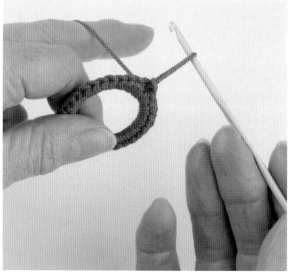

**yarn round hook** 🔲 and pull through loop on hook, * insert hook in ring, pull loop through, yarn round hook, pull through 2 loops (1 **double crochet** 🔟 made).

**Fasten off** 🔲 , leaving an end to sew with. Thread this end on to wool needle and join by taking it over the first dc of the round, under the two top strands of the next dc, then back into the last dc of the round, so that it looks like the top of a dc. **Darn in** 🔲 the first end, but leave the second free. Cover remaining large rings with B, C and A.

## Tie

With C, cover 1 small ring with 20 dc, or required number of stitches, **slip stitch 7** to first dc, make 150 **chain 6** , 20 dc, or required number, around second small ring,

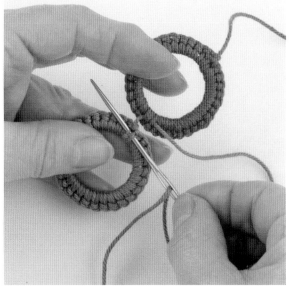

slip stitch to first dc.
Fasten off.

## Finishing

Join two large rings by using the free end of one to stitch, on the wrong side, to a point opposite the free end of the second. Continue joining the rings in this way, then **darn in 24** the last end.
Thread the tie through the end rings.

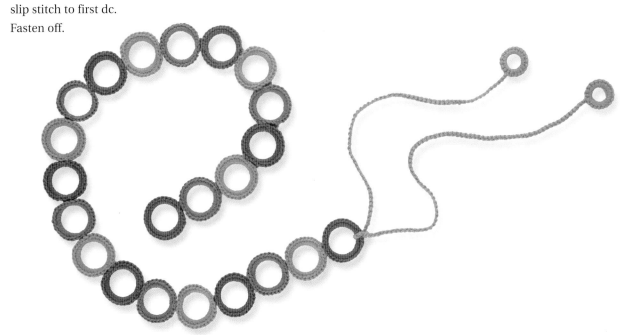

# 2 Treble

Treble is a taller stitch than double crochet, allowing more freedom to make open textures as well as fast-growing fabrics. You just have to remember to take the yarn round before inserting the hook, then everything follows logically. These projects are very varied but only hint at the possibilities that treble crochet has to offer.

# Striped Scarf

This long fringed scarf is made very special with the use of a sleek luxury yarn in wonderful rich colours.

The foundation chain is worked with a size larger hook to avoid puckering. Then each stripe is one row of treble and the fringe is attached with the crochet hook.

## You will need

5 x 50g balls Debbie Bliss Cathay:
  2 balls purple (A)
  2 balls shocking pink (B)
  1 ball orange (C)
4.50mm hook
5.00mm hook

## Size

9cm x 128cm (3½in x 51in) plus fringe

## Tension

16 sts and 10 rows to 10cm (4in) over tr with the 4.50mm hook

## Abbreviations

ch – chain; cm – centimetres; in – inches; st(s) – stitch(es); tr – treble

# MAKING THE SCARF

With 5.00mm hook and A, make 206 **chain 6** .
Change to 4.50mm hook.

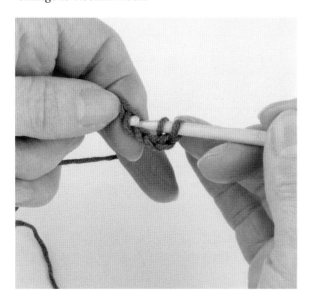

**ROW 1**  Miss 3 ch.
* 1 **treble 11** in next ch;

**ROW 2**  With B, 3 ch,

* 1 tr in next tr;
repeat from * to last st,

repeat from * to end. 204 sts.

1 tr in top ch of 3 ch.

ROW 3  With A, 3 ch, * 1 tr in next tr; repeat from * to last st, 1 tr in top ch of 3 ch.

ROW 4  As row 2.

ROW 5  As row 3.

ROW 6  As row 2.

ROW 7  As row 3.

ROW 8  As row 2.

ROW 9  With C, as row 2.

**Fasten off 21 .**

## Finishing

Lightly damp press.

Fringe the ends, matching each tassel to a stripe. A tassel consists of 5 strands of yarn, each strand approximately 30cm (12in) long.

Double the 5 strands and then hook them through a row end to make a loop.

Hook the ends through the loop and pull up firmly. Comb the fringe to separate the individual strands within the yarn.

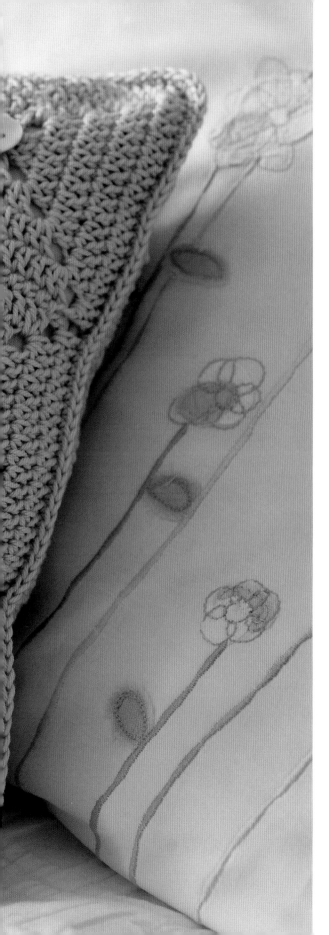

# Cushion With Buttons

Achieve a quilted look by adding a mother-of-pearl button to the centre of each square of a pastel-coloured patchwork.

The first pieced project, this cushion is made up of squares made with chain and treble, then joined with double crochet on the wrong side.

## You will need

5 x 50g balls Jaeger Aqua in grey-blue
3.00mm hook
9 mother-of-pearl buttons
Cushion pad

## Size

Approximately 29cm x 29cm (11½ in x 11½ in)

## Tension

Each square measures approximately 9cm (3½in) with 3.00mm hook

## Abbreviations

ch – chain; ch sp – chain space; cm – centimetres; dc – double crochet; in – inches; sp – space; ss – slip stitch; tr – treble

# MAKING THE CUSHION

## Square

(make 18)

Make 5 **chain** `6` , **slip stitch** `7` into first ch to form a **ring** `9` .

Working in **rounds** `14` with right side facing:

**ROUND 1** 3 ch, 2 **treble** `11` in ring, 3 ch, * 3 tr in ring, 3 ch;

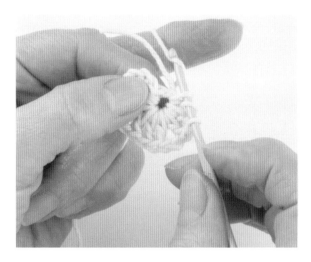

rep from * twice, ss to top ch of 3 ch.

**ROUND 2** 3 ch,

1 tr in each of next 2 tr, (2 tr, 3 ch, 2 tr) in ch sp, * 1 tr in each of next 3 tr, (2 tr, 3 ch, 2 tr) in ch sp; rep from * twice, ss to top ch of 3 ch.

**ROUND 3** 3 ch, 1 tr in each of next 4 tr, (2 tr, 3 ch, 2 tr) in ch sp, * 1 tr in each of next 7 tr, (2 tr, 3 ch, 2 tr) in ch sp; rep from * twice, 1 tr in each of next 2 tr, ss to top ch of 3 ch.

**ROUND 4** 3 ch, 1 tr in each of next 6 tr, (2 tr, 3 ch, 2 tr) in ch sp, * 1 tr in each of next 11 tr, (2 tr, 3 ch, 2 tr) in ch sp; rep from * twice, 1 tr in each of next 4 tr, ss to top ch of 3 ch.

**Fasten off** `21` .

## Finishing

Set out two blocks of 9 squares each, the joins of each round facing in the same direction.

With right sides together, take 2 squares and **join with double crochet** `22`: insert the hook under 2 strands of the first tr of 15 tr of front square and

under 2 strands of the corresponding tr of the back square, yarn round hook, and pull through a loop, yarn round hook again and pull it through 2 loops to make a dc.

Joining only the groups of 15 tr, join the remaining 7 squares of the back in the same way, then join the 9 squares of the front.

## Edging

Back: with right side facing, **join the yarn** [20] at one corner and work

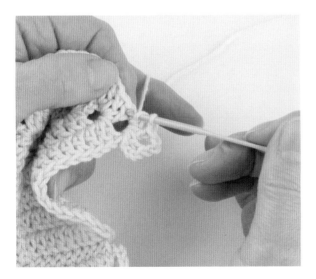

(3 ch, 1 tr, 3 ch, 2 tr) in corner sp, * 1 tr in each of next 15 tr, [2 tr in last sp of this motif, 1 ch, 2 tr in first sp

of next motif, 1 tr in each of next 15 tr] twice, (2 tr, 3 ch, 2 tr) in corner sp; rep from * along each side, joining last side to first with ss in top ch of 3 ch. Edge the front to match.
Fasten off.

Press to shape.
Take the back and front and join with dc: wrong sides together and working through 2 strands of each pair of stitches, work (1 ch, 2 dc) in one corner sp, * 1 dc in each of next 19 tr, 1 dc in 1-ch sp; rep from * once, 1 dc in each of next 19 tr, 3 dc in corner sp. Continue in this way along 2 more sides, working 3 dc in corners, to the last side and work into the front only along this side to leave an opening for the cushion pad, ss to 1 ch.
Fasten off.
Sew a button to the centre of each square of the front.
Insert the cushion pad and stitch the opening closed.

# Baby's Garland

Friendly teddy bear faces and colourful pompons should enchant a very young baby.

Rounds of treble make all the crochet components of the teddies. Minimal sewing and embroidery skills are needed to complete the project.

## You will need

3 x 50g balls Jaeger Matchmaker Double Knitting:
    1 ball camel (A)
    1 ball chocolate (B)
    1 ball turquoise (C)
3.00mm hook
Small quantity of wadding
Wool needle
Ribbon

## Size

Approximately 28cm (11in) long, including pompons

## Tension

9 sts and 5 rows to 5cm (2in) over tr with 3.00mm hook

## Abbreviations

ch – chain; cm – centimetres; in – inches; ss – slip stitch; sts – stitches; tr – treble

# MAKING THE GARLAND

## Bear head

(make 2 pieces for each bear)

**ROUND 1** With A, make a **slip ring** 🔢, 3 **chain** 6️⃣, 11 **treble** 🔢 in ring,

pull ring tight, ss to top ch of 3 ch. 12 sts. **

**ROUND 2** 3 ch, 1 tr in ss of round 1, [2 tr in next tr] 11 times, ss to top ch of 3 ch.  24 sts.

**ROUND 3** 3 ch, 2 tr in next tr,

[1 tr in next tr, 2 tr in next tr] 11 times, ss to top ch of 3 ch.  36 sts.

**Fasten off** 🔢 .

## Muzzle and ears

(make 3 pieces for each bear)

With A, work as head to **. Fasten off, leaving an end long enough to sew with.

## Finishing

Push centre of muzzle forward and coil first end inside to pad it. Place muzzle, its join downward, just below centre of one head piece, also join downward.

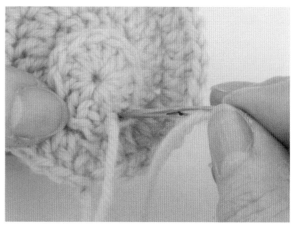

Use second end to stab stitch it in place along inner edge of top 2 strands of each stitch.

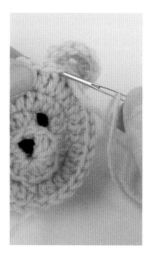

With B, embroider nose in satin stitch and eyes with French knots.

Stab stitch ears to face. Place face on back head piece and stab stitch the front and back together.

Push wadding into the head before completing.

## Pompons

With C, make pompons: cut 2 discs of card with a hole in the centre and put one on top of the other.

Cut around the edge. Slip a length of yarn between the discs and tie, sliding out the discs and leaving ends long enough to sew with. Take the ends through each head just below the ears and secure with a few back stitches.

Attach ribbons at each end of the garland.

Wrap round both with yarn until full.

# Hippy Handbag

Sling it over your shoulder or use it as a decorative hold-all around the home. Enjoy the off-beat colours used here or design your own palette.

These squares mix chain, double crochet and treble in a project that's entirely crochet – no sewing is needed at all.

## You will need

7 x 50g balls Rowan Cotton Glace:

    1 ball green (A)
    1 ball turquoise (B)
    1 ball lilac (C)
    1 ball yellow (D
    1 ball blue (E)
    2 balls purple (F)

2.50mm hook

## Size

Approximately 23cm x 23cm (9in x 9in)

## Tension

One square measures 7.5cm (3in) with 2.50mm hook

## Abbreviations

ch – chain; ch sp – chain space; cm – centimetres; dc – double crochet; in – inches; sp – space; ss – slip stitch; st(s) – stitch(es); tr – treble

# MAKING THE HANDBAG

## Square

(make 18)

With A, make 6 **chain** ,

ss into first ch to form a **ring** . Work in **rounds** with right side facing:

**ROUND 1** 3 ch, 15 **treble** in ring, **slip stitch** to top ch of 3 ch.
16 sts.

**ROUND 2** 4 ch, [1 tr in next tr, 1 ch] 15 times,

ss to 3rd of 4 ch.
**Fasten off** A.

**ROUND 3** **Join new yarn** . With B, pull loop through a ch sp,

then work (3 ch, 2 tr) in that sp, 3 tr in each of next 15 ch sp, ss to top ch of 3 ch. Fasten off B.

**ROUND 4** With C, pull loop through a sp between tr groups and work 4 ch, 1 **double crochet** in next sp between tr groups [3 ch, 1 dc in next sp between tr groups] twice, * 5 ch, 1 dc in next sp between tr groups, [3 ch, 1 dc in next sp between tr groups] 3 times; rep from * twice more, 4 ch,

ss to first of first 4 ch.

**ROUND 5** 1 ch, 2 dc in first ch sp, 3 dc in each of next 2 ch sp, * (3 dc, 2 ch, 3 dc) in corner sp,

3 dc in each of next 3 ch sp; rep from * twice more, (3 dc, 2 ch, 3 dc) in corner sp, ss to 1 ch.
Fasten off C.
Make 17 more squares, bringing in D and E. In some squares substitute F for C in rounds 4 and 5.

## Handles

(make 2)

With F, make 150 ch.

Miss 2 ch, 1 dc in each ch to end, 2 ch, without turning work over,

work 1 dc in each remaining strand of foundation ch. Fasten off.

## Finishing

Press the squares to shape.

Assemble the squares in a rectangle, 3 across and 6 down.

With right sides together, **join 2 squares with double crochet** 22: with F, begin at corner 2-ch sp, insert hook under strands of first front edge stitch and strands of corresponding back edge stitch, yarn round hook and pull through a loop, yarn round hook again and pull it through 2 loops to make a dc.

Continue to join each pair of edge sts in this way, then, without fastening off, join the next pair of

squares in the same way. When all rows across have been completed, join the long rows to complete the rectangle.

Fold the rectangle, wrong sides together, join side seams with dc: with F, working 1 dc in a pair of front and back sts each time.

### Top edging

Working in rounds with right side facing:

ROUND 1 Starting at a side seam and using F, pull through a loop, ** 1 ch, * 1 dc in next st;

repeat from * around front and back of bag, ss to 1 ch.

ROUND 2 As round 1 from **.

Fasten off.

Sew on handles.

# Slot-through Scarf

If the motif looks familiar that's because the granny square, as it's sometimes called, is one of the most enduring crochet designs around.

Groups of treble and a few chain make up the square motifs. They're joined with double crochet and edged with picots – decorative little blips which are simply 3 chain with a double crochet in the first chain.

## You will need

6 x 50g balls Rowan 4 ply Soft:
  1 ball pink (A)
  1 ball lilac (B)
  1 ball  lime (C
  1 ball  turquoise (D)
  2 balls grey (E)
2.50mm hook

## Size

Approximately 13cm (5in) wide x 78cm (30in) long

## Tension

One square measures approximately 5cm (2in) with 2.50mm hook

## Abbreviations

ch – chain; ch sp – chain space; cm – centimetres; dc – double crochet; in – inches; sp – space; ss – slip stitch; tr – treble

# MAKING THE SCARF

## Square

(make 30)

With A, make 5 **chain** 6 , **slip stitch** 7 into first ch to form a **ring** 9 . Work in **rounds** 14 with the right side facing:

**ROUND 1** 3 ch, 2 **treble** 11 in ring, 2 ch, *3 tr, 2 ch; rep from * twice,

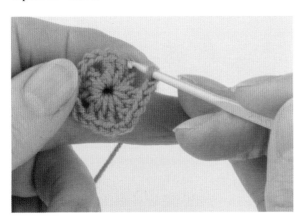

ss to top ch of 3 ch. **Fasten off** 21 .

**ROUND 2** With B, **join yarn** 20 in first ch sp by pulling through a loop and then in same ch sp work (3 ch, 2 tr, 2 ch, 3 tr), *in next ch sp work (3 tr, 2 ch, 3 tr); rep from * twice,

ss to top ch of 3 ch.
Fasten off.

**ROUND 3** With E, join yarn in first ch sp of this round as before, in same ch sp work (3 ch, 2 tr, 2 ch, 3 tr), in sp between groups work 3 tr, * in next ch sp work (3 tr, 2 ch, 3 tr), in sp between groups work 3 tr; rep from * twice, ss to top ch of 3 ch.

Fasten off.

Make 29 more squares, repeating this colour combination and substituting other colours for A and B, but always working round 3 with E.

## Finishing

Press squares to shape.

Assemble scarf in 2 rows of 15 squares.

With right sides together and using E, take the first pair of squares and **join with double crochet** 22 : inserting the hook under the inner strand only of each pair of stitches, work 1 dc in corner ch,

1 dc in each of 9 tr, 1 dc in next corner ch.
Fasten off.

Join additional squares in the same way until there are
2 strips of 15 squares each. Join the long centre seam in
the same way, leaving an opening between squares on
the fourth row from one end. With right side facing and
using E, work a row of dc along the 2 sides of this
opening.

## Edging

ROUND 1 Working in rounds with right side facing:
With E, join yarn to the first corner ch of a square
roughly midway along a 15-row edge, 1 ch,
1 dc in each of 9 tr, * 1 dc in next corner ch, 1 tr in
seam between squares, 1 dc in next corner ch, 1 dc in
each of 9 tr 2; rep from * to corner of scarf,

(2 dc in first ch, 1 dc in 2nd ch), then continue in this
way around the sides and into corners of scarf,
ending ss to 1 ch.
ROUND 2 1 ch, 1 dc in next dc, * 3 ch,

1 dc in first of 3 ch (picot made), 1 dc in each of next
3 dc; rep from * around scarf, ending 3 ch, 1 dc in
first of 3 ch, join with ss to 1 ch.
Fasten off.

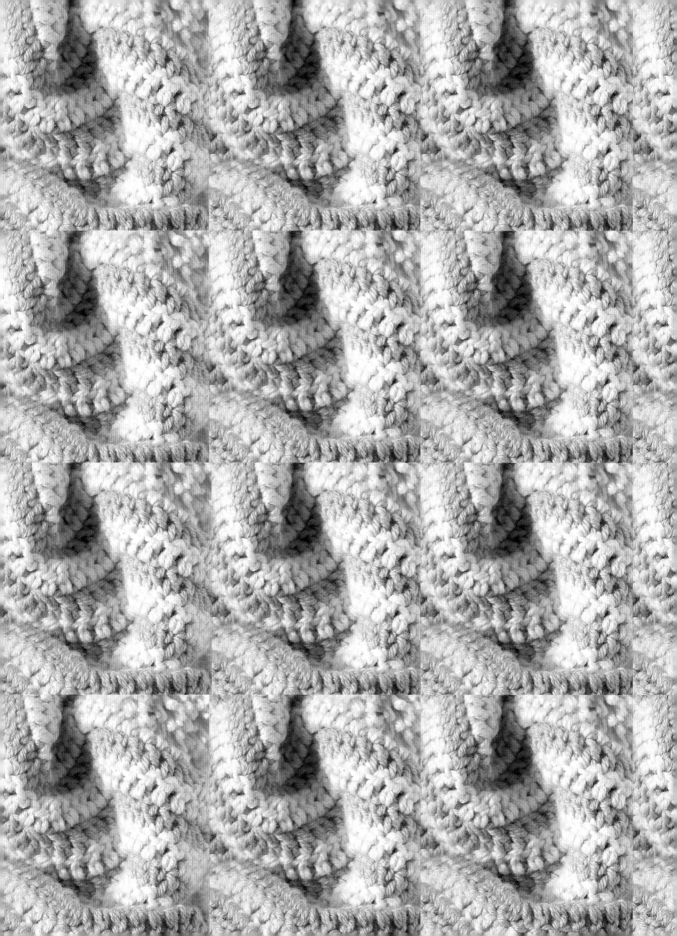

# 3

# Shaping

Crochet is a wonderfully creative medium because there's no need for seams, no limit to the length of a row or a round and there's a multitude of effects you can achieve with increases and decreases.

If 'made' stitches (increases) are balanced by 'lost' stitches (decreases) the crochet is patterned but remains flat. Increases or decreases used alone will shape the fabric into curves, either at the edges or all over.

# Hat With Brim

Wear this classic hat whichever way suits you best – with the brim turned back or right down over your eyes.

All the shapings are increases, which are very easy – they're simply two stitches instead of one. The rounds are continuous so it's best to use a marker of contrast yarn to keep count of stitches and rounds.

## You will need

2 x 50g balls Jaeger Matchmaker Merino Aran
    in turquoise
5.50mm hook
6.00mm hook
Short length of contrast yarn for marker

## Size
To fit average adult

## Tension
12 sts and 16 rows to 10cm (4in) over dc with 6.00mm hook

## Abbreviations
ch – chain; cm – centimetres; dc – double crochet; in – inches;

# MAKING THE HAT

**ROUND 1** Make a **slip ring** 16.
With 6.00mm hook, 2 **chain** 6, 11 **double crochet** 10 in ring,

Insert **yarn marker** 15 before starting each round. The illustration shows the yarn marker lying between rounds.

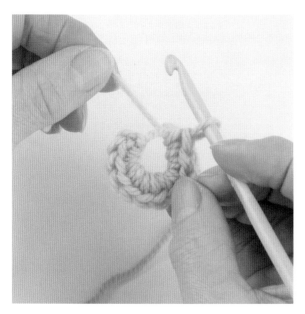

pull ring tight, **slip stitch** 7 to top ch of 2 ch. 12 sts. Keeping the right side facing, work in **rounds** 14.

The illustration shows an increase being made by working 2 dc into 1 dc.

**ROUND 2** 1 dc in top ch of 2 ch, 2 dc in first dc of round 1, [1 dc in next dc, 2 dc in next dc] 5 times. 18 dc.

**ROUND 3** [1 dc in next dc, 2 dc in next dc] 9 times. 27 dc.

**ROUND 4** 1 dc in each dc.

**ROUND 5** [1 dc in each of next 2 dc, 2 dc in next dc] 9 times. 36 dc.

**ROUNDS 6 AND 7** As round 4.

**ROUND 8** [1 dc in each of next 2 dc, 2 dc in next dc] 12 times. 48 dc.

**ROUNDS 9, 10 AND 11** As round 4.

**ROUND 12** [1 dc in each of next 2 dc, 2 dc in next dc] 16 times. 64 dc.

**ROUNDS 13 TO 24** As round 4.

**ROUND 25** [1 dc in each of next 3 dc, 2 dc in next dc] 16 times. 80 dc.

**ROUNDS 26 TO 29** As round 4.

**ROUND 30** [1 dc in each of next 7 dc, 2 dc in next dc] 10 times. 90 dc.

**ROUNDS 31 TO 33** As round 4.

**ROUND 34** With 5.50mm hook, work 1 dc around each dc (that is, work into the round below instead of the top of the stitch).

**Fasten off** **21**.

Pull out marker, **darn in ends** **24**.

# Pet Ball

Make a small, soft ball in double crochet as an indoor toy for a pampered pet.

Rounds of increases are matched by rounds of decreases to create a sphere. If it isn't perfectly round this can be corrected with firm stuffing!

## You will need

1 x 50g ball Debbie Bliss Merino DK in lime
4.00mm hook
Filling
Short length of contrast yarn for marker
Wool needle

## Size
Circumference approximately 21cm (8½in)

## Tension
9 sts and 10 rows to 5cm (2in) over dc with the 4.00mm hook

## Abbreviations
ch – chain; cm – centimetres; dc – double crochet; dec in next 2 dc – decrease one st: [insert hook in next dc, yarn round hook and pull loop through] twice, yarn round hook and pull it through all 3 loops; in – inches; st(s) – stitch(es)

# MAKING THE BALL

Working in **rounds** 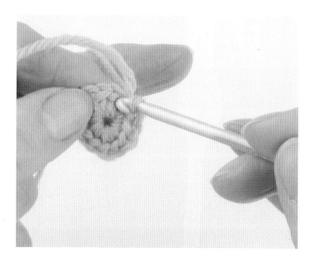 with right side facing:

**ROUND 1** Make a **slip ring** 🔟, 2 **chain** **6**, 11 **double crochet** **10** in ring, pull ring tight,

**slip stitch** **7** to top ch of 2 ch. 12 sts.

Insert **yarn marker** 🔟 before starting next and every round.

**ROUND 2** 1 dc in top ch of 2 ch, 2 dc in first dc, [1 dc in next dc,

2 dc in next dc] 5 times. 18 dc.

**ROUND 3** [1 dc in each of next 2 dc, 2 dc in next dc] 6 times. 24 dc.

**ROUND 4** 1 dc in each of 24 dc.

**ROUND 5** [1 dc in each of next 3 dc, 2 dc in next dc] 6 times. 30 dc.

**ROUNDS 6 AND 7** 1 dc in each of 30 dc.

**ROUND 8** [1 dc in each of next 4 dc, 2 dc in next dc] 6 times. 36 dc.

**ROUNDS 9, 10, 11 AND 12** 1 dc in each of 36 dc.

**ROUND 13** [1 dc in each of next 4 dc, 1 **decrease** 🔟 in next 2 dc] 6 times. 30 dc.

**ROUNDS 14 AND 15** As round 6.

**ROUND 16** [1 dc in each of next 3 dc, 1 dec in next 2 dc] 6 times. 24 dc.

**ROUND 17** As round 4.

**ROUND 18** [1 dc in each of next 2 dc, 1 dec in next 2 dc] 6 times. 18 dc.

**ROUND 19** [1 dc in next dc, 1 dec in next 2 dc] 6 times. 12 dc.

## Finishing

Pull out marker and complete filling.
Thread end of yarn on to wool needle and use to
gather up last 6 sts and then

oversew to match the other side of the ball.

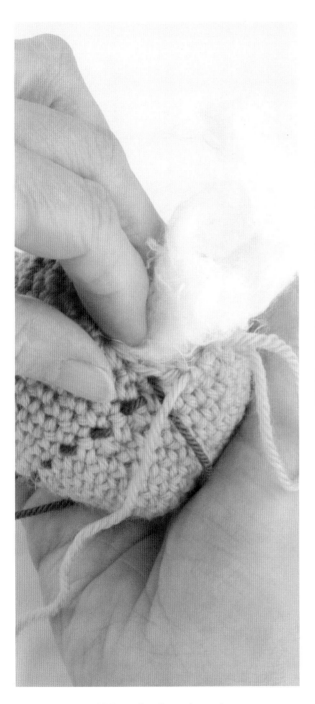

Push in most of filling, firmly and evenly.

**ROUND 20** [1 dec in next 2 dc] 6 times.  6 dc.

**Fasten off 21 .**

# Rose

Instead of a brooch, pin a bold crochet
rose to your jacket or jumper.

The flower is made in one strip. A row of
treble has treble and double treble scallops
worked along it and is then gathered up.
The stem is chain with slip stitch.

## You will need

1 x 50g ball of Jaeger Extra Fine Merino DK in pink
4.00mm hook
Wool needle

## Size

Approximately 7.5cm (3in) across

## Tension

9 sts to 5cm (2in) over tr with 4.00mm hook

## Abbreviations

ch – chain; cm – centimetres; d tr – double treble:
yarn round hook twice, insert hook into next stitch,
yarn round hook, pull through a loop to make 4
loops on hook [yarn round hook, pull it through next
2 loops] 3 times; in – inches; ss – slip stitch;
sts – stitches; tr – treble

# MAKING THE ROSE

Leaving a fairly long end, make 71 **chain** **6** .
**ROW 1** Miss 3 ch, 1 **treble** **11** in each ch to end.
69 sts.

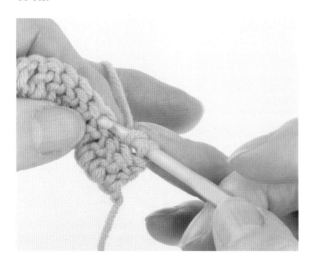

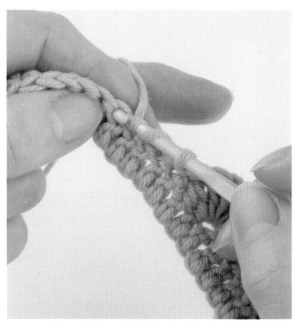

**ROW 2** [Miss next 2 tr.
7 tr in next tr, miss next 2 tr,

7 **double treble** (see abbreviations on page 72) in next tr, miss next 3 tr,

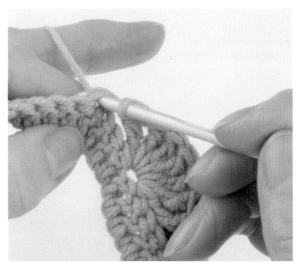

ss in next tr] 4 times, miss next 3 tr, 7 d tr in next tr, miss next 2 tr, ss in top ch of 3 ch. 5 small petals and 5 larger petals made.
**Fasten off** **21** , leaving an end of wool long enough to sew with.

**slip stitch** **7** in next tr] 5 times,
[miss next 3 tr,

## Finishing

### Rose

Thread first end on to a wool needle and

run it under and over remaining strands of
base chain.

Pull up to gather.

Starting with smaller petals, coil the strip, tightly at
first and then more loosely, the spaces between petals
alternating as far as possible. Stitch base of petals,
using second end of yarn.

### Stem

Make 16 ch, miss 1 ch,

ss in each ch to end.

Fasten off, leaving an end long enough to sew the
stem on with.

# Zig Zag Hat

Stripes are more interesting when they run in chevrons around a baby's hat.

Increases and decreases along the row cause the stripes to zigzag and the edge to wave. But these are all the shapings involved in this pattern, there's no shaping in the crown of the hat – the chevrons are pleated at the top.

## You will need

2 x 50g balls of Rowan Wool Cotton:
   1 ball turquoise (A)
   1 ball lime (B)
3.50mm hook
4.50mm hook
Wool needle

## Size

To fit a child age 6–9 months

## Tension

14 sts (one repeat) and 7 rows to 7cm (3in) over tr with 3.50mm hook

## Abbreviations

ch – chain; cm – centimetres; double dec – double decrease: [yarn round hook, insert hook in next stitches, yarn round hook and pull loop through, yarn round hook and pull it through 2 loops on hook] 3 times, yarn round hook and pull it through all 4 loops on hook; in – inches; tr – treble; st(s) – stitch(es).

# MAKING THE HAT

With 4.50mm hook and A, make 73 **chain** **6**.
Change to 3.50mm hook.

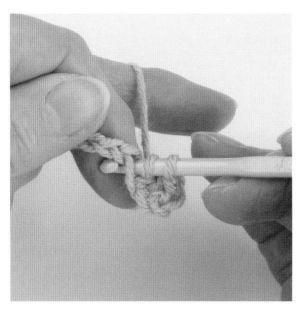

**ROW 1** Miss 3 ch, 2 **treble** **11** in next ch,
1 tr in each of next 4 ch,

[**double decrease** (see abbreviations on page 82) in
next 3 ch, 1 tr in each of next 5 ch,

3 tr in next ch, 1 tr in each of next 5 ch] 4 times,
double dec in next 3 ch, 1 tr in each of next 5 ch,

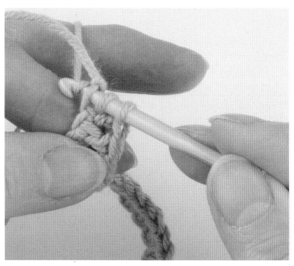

2 tr in last ch. 71 sts.
**ROW 2** With B, 3 ch, 1 tr in st below, 1 tr in each of
next 5 sts, [double dec in next 3 sts, 1 tr in each of
next 5 sts, 3 tr in next st, 1 tr in each of next 5 sts]
4 times, double dec in next 3 sts, 1 tr in each of next
5 sts, 2 tr in top ch of 3 ch.

**ROW 3** With A, as row 2.

Repeat rows 2 and 3
9 times.

**Fasten off 21 .**

## Finishing

On the wrong side at the top, pinch the V-shaped
chevrons to form folds. Stitch each pair of edges,
taking in both strands of each stitch. When all five
chevrons are joined, sew about half of the back seam
on the wrong side from the top, then reverse the
seam for the turn-back cuff.

Make a pompon (see page 59) with B and attach to
the top of the hat.

# Baby Brogues

These quirky little shoes would make a perfect present for a young baby.

There's quite a lot of shaping involved in making the curves, but the project is tiny and there's almost no sewing required.

## You will need

1 a 50g ball of Jaeger Matchmaker Merino Aran
    in dusky pink
4.50mm hook
Short length of contrast yarn for marker
Wool needle
Ribbon

## Size
To fit 0–3 months

## Tension
7 sts and 9 rows to 5cm (2in) over dc with 4.50mm hook

## Abbreviations
ch – chain; ch sp – chain space; cm – centimetres; dc – double crochet; dec in next 2 dc – decrease one st: [insert hook in next dc, yarn round hook and pull loop through] twice, yarn round hook and pull it through all 3 loops on hook; in – inches; ss – slip stitch; sp – space; st(s) – stitch(es)

# MAKING THE SHOES

## Main part

(starting with the sole)

Make 8 **chain** 6.

Work in **rounds** 14 with right side facing:

**ROUND 1** Miss 3 ch,

1 **double crochet** 10 in each of 5 ch, 2 ch, without turning work over, 1 dc in each remaining single strand of 5 ch, 1 dc in next ch, 2 ch, ss to next ch.

Insert **yarn marker** 15 before starting next and following rounds.

**ROUND 2** 1 dc in next ch, 1 dc in each of next 5 dc, 3 dc in 2-ch sp, 1 dc in each of next 6 dc, 3 dc in 2-ch sp. 18 dc.

**ROUND 3** [1 dc in each of next 6 dc, 2 dc in each of next 3 dc] twice. 24 dc.

**ROUND 4** [1 dc in each of next 6 dc,

2 dc in each of next 6 dc] twice. 36 dc.

**ROUNDS 5 AND 6** 1 dc in each dc.

**ROUND 7** [1 dc in each of next 2 dc, dec in next 2 dc, 1 dc in each of next 2 dc] 6 times. 30 dc. Work 1 dc in each of next 3 dc beyond marker.

Turn and now work in **rows** 12 for back extension:

**ROW 1** (wrong side) 1 ch, 1 dc in dc below, 1 dc in each of next 10 dc, 2 dc in next dc, turn. 14 sts.

**ROWS 2 TO 8** 1 ch, 1 dc in each of next 12 dc, 1 dc in ch.

**Fasten off** 21, leaving an end of yarn long enough to sew with.

## Top

(worked in rounds like the sole)

Make 5 chain.

**ROUND 1** Miss 3 ch, 1 dc in each of 2 ch, 2 ch, 1 dc in each remaining single strand of 2 base ch, 1 dc in next ch, 2 ch, ss in next ch of 3 ch.

Insert yarn marker before starting next and following rounds.

**ROUND 2** 1 dc in ch, 1 dc in each of next 2 dc, 3 dc in 2-ch sp, 1 dc in each of next 3 dc, 3 dc in 2-ch sp. 12 sts.

**ROUND 3** [1 dc in each of next 3 dc, 2 dc in each of next 3 dc] twice. 18 dc.

**ROUND 4** 1 dc in each of next 3 dc, 2 dc in each of next 6 dc] twice. 30 dc. Work 1 dc in each of next 2 dc beyond marker. Do not fasten off.

## Finishing

Take top and main part and **join with double crochet 22:** wrong sides together, place top on main part of shoe and, starting beside back extension and using attached yarn,

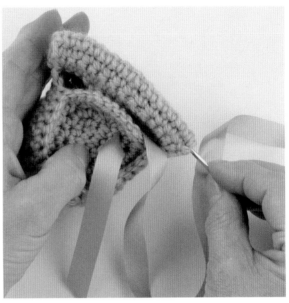

insert hook under both strands of next dc of top and next dc of main part, yarn round hook, pull loop through, yarn round hook and pull it through both loops on hook to complete a dc. Continue in this way until 18 pairs of stitches have been joined. Fasten off.

Thread ribbon through the casing and bring the ends out through the stitches of the top front. Tie in a bow and trim the ends.

Fold back extension in half to the right side and stitch it down along the edge to make a casing.

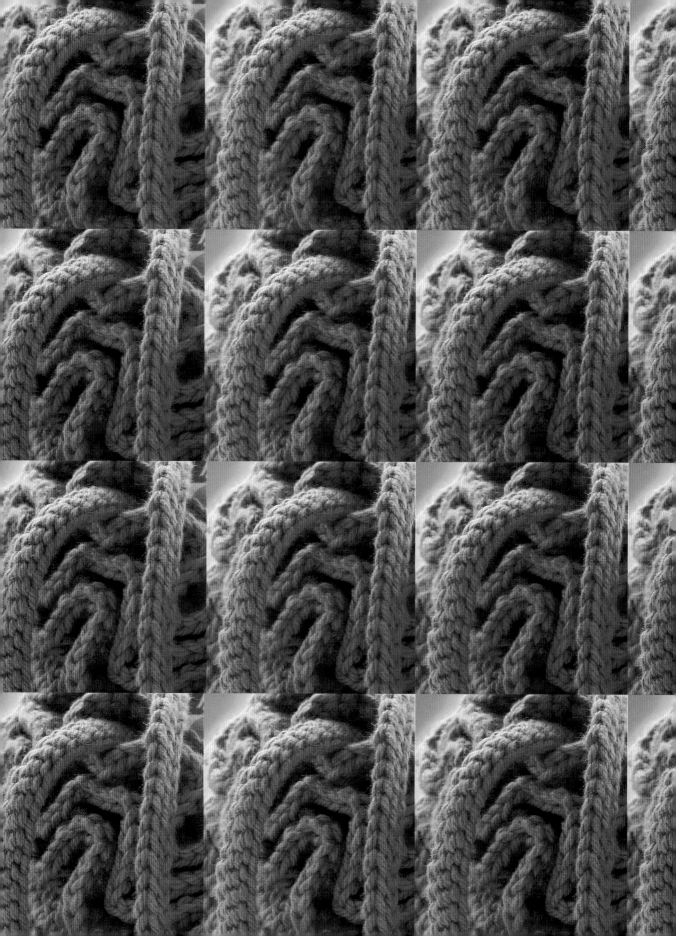

# 4

# Special Effects

Still using simple stitches, but in new combinations, these designs explore some new directions in crochet. Some are larger-scale projects than before, others include double treble which, as its name suggests, is a variation on treble. They all require a little confidence and good basic skills.

# String Bag

Sturdy denim yarn makes this a user-friendly update on the old-fashioned string bag.

The main part is an easy mesh pattern of chain and double crochet, starting from a circular base and finishing with double crochet.

## You will need

2 x 50g balls Rowan Denim in pale blue
3.50mm hook

## Size

Approximately 25cm (10in) wide and 28cm (11in) long

## Tension

Based on a tension of 4 mesh to 10cm (4in) with 3.50mm hook

## Abbreviations

ch – chain; ch sp – chain space; cm – centimetres; dc – double crochet; in – inches; tr – treble; ss – slip stitch; st(s) – stitch(es)

# MAKING THE BAG

Make 6 **chain** 6 , ss in first ch to join into a **ring** 9 .
ROUND 1  4 ch, [1 **treble** 11 in ring, 1 ch] 11 times,
ss in 3rd of 4 ch,

ss in next ch sp.
Now you have 12 chain spaces.

ROUND 2  [2 ch, 1 **double crochet** 10 in next ch sp]
11 times, 1 ch, 1 dc in first of 2 ch.
ROUND 3  [3 ch, 1 dc in next ch sp] 11 times, 2 ch, 1 dc
in first of 3 ch.
ROUND 4  [4 ch, 1 dc in next ch sp] 11 times, 3 ch, 1 dc
in first of 4 ch.
ROUND 5  [5 ch, 1 dc in next ch sp] 11 times, 2 ch, 1 tr
in first of 5 ch.
ROUND 6  [6 ch, 1 dc in next ch sp] 11 times, 3 ch, 1 tr
in first of 6 ch.

ROUND 7  [6 ch, (1 dc, 6 ch, 1 dc) in next ch sp, 6 ch, 1
dc in next ch sp] 5 times, 6 ch, (1 dc, 6 ch,
1 dc) in next ch sp, 3 ch,

1 tr in first of 6 ch.
18 ch sp.
ROUND 8  [6 ch,1 dc in next ch sp] 17 times, 3 ch, 1 tr
in first of 6 ch.
ROUND 9  [6 ch, (1 dc, 6 ch, 1 dc) in next ch sp, (6 ch,
1 dc) in each of next 2 ch sp] 5 times, 6 ch, (1 dc, 6 ch,
1 dc) in next ch sp, 6 ch, 1 dc in next ch sp, 3 ch, 1 tr
in first of 6 ch.  24 ch sp.
ROUND 10  [6 ch, 1 dc in next ch sp] 23 times, 3 ch, 1 tr
in first of 6 ch.
Repeat last round 18 times.

ROUND 29  [3 ch, 1 dc in next ch sp] 23 times, 3 ch,
ss in first of 3 ch].

## Finishing

**Edging**

ROUND 30 1 ch,

[3 dc in 3-ch sp, 1 dc in dc] 23 times, 3 dc in 3-ch sp, ss in 1 ch. 96 sts.

ROUND 31 1 ch, 1 dc in each dc, ending ss in 1 ch. Do not break yarn.

## Handles

First handle ** 52 ch, turn, miss 1 ch,

1 dc in each ch, ss into nearest dc of edging, 2 ch, turn so that 2 ch lie to inside of bag, ss into dc of edging nearest other side of handle, half turn, along second side of handle,

work 1 dc in remaining strand of each dc.

**Fasten off 21 ,** leaving end long enough to stitch this part of handle to bag.

Second handle: on opposite side of bag, right side facing, ss into 1 dc of edging, work as first handle from **.

Without twisting them, sew remaining ends of handles to edging.

# Ribbed Cushion

Strongly-defined ribs give this simple cushion its firm fabric and bold texture.

The ribs are made by working double trebles over and around stitches. This is one of those techniques that is much easier than it looks and the patterning is only done on the right side.

## You will need

10 x 50g balls Debbie Bliss Cotton DK
4.00mm hook
Cushion pad

## Size

Approximately 35cm x 35cm (14in x 14in)

## Tension

16 sts and 13 rows to 10cm (4in) over pattern with 4.00mm hook

## Abbreviations

ch – chain; cm – centimetres; dc – double crochet; d tr b – double treble made around a stitch 2 rows below: yarn round hook twice, miss dc row below, insert hook under next stitch of row below from right to left, bringing hook out on right side, yarn round hook, pull through loop (4 loops on hook), [yarn round hook, pull it through 2 loops] 3 times;
in – inches; ss – slip stitch; st(s) – stitch(es); tr – treble

# MAKING THE CUSHION

## Back

With 4.00mm hook, make 57 **chain** **6**.

**ROW 1** (right side) Miss 3 ch,

[1 **treble** **11** in next ch] 54 times. 55 sts.

**ROW 2** 1 ch,

[1 **double crochet** **10** in next tr] 53 times, 1 dc in top ch of 3 ch.

**ROW 3** 3 ch, 1 tr in next dc,

1 **double treble below** (see abbreviations on page 97) around 3rd st of first row, [1 tr in next dc, 1 d tr b in next but one tr of first row] 25 times, 1 tr in next dc, 1 tr in 1 ch.

**ROW 4** 1 ch, [1 dc in next st] 53 times, 1 dc in top ch of 3 ch.

**ROW 5** 3 ch, 1 tr in next dc,

1 d tr b around first d tr b, [1 tr in next but one dc of last row, 1 d tr b around next d tr b] 25 times, 1 tr in next but one dc of last row, 1 tr in ch.

**ROWS 4 AND 5** form pattern.

Repeat rows 4 and 5 another 21 times, thus ending with a right side row.

Do not fasten off.

## Edging

**ROUND 1** With right side facing, (1 ch, 2 dc) in first corner, working under two strands of yarn each time work 1 dc in each dc and 2 dc in each tr of first side, 3 dc in corner,1 dc in each remaining strand of base ch, 3 dc in corner, third side as opposite side,

3 dc in corner, 1 dc in each st of fourth side, ss to 1 ch.

## Front

Work as back.

## Finishing

Place back and front with wrong sides together, **join with double crochet 22**: 1 ch, insert hook under both strands of first st of front and both strands of first st of back, make a dc in the usual way, continue to make 1 dc in each pair of sts and 3 dc in the centre dc at each corner to the last side. Insert the cushion pad and complete the round with ss to 1 ch.

**Fasten off 21 .**

# Clothes Cover

Open effects can appear rather daunting to a beginner, but this chunky edging is quite simple and could be put to all kinds of uses around the home.

It's worked repeat-by-repeat lengthways so you simply stop when you have the length you require. The ring that starts the repeat is joined with a double treble but that's the only unusual feature of the stitch pattern.

## You will need

1 x 100g ball of Sirdar Pure Cotton DK in white
3.50mm hook
Cotton or linen fabric, paper, sewing thread
Wooden coat hanger

## Tension

1 pattern measures approximately 4cm (1½ in) long with 3.50mm hook

## Abbreviations

ch – chain; cm – centimetres; dc – double crochet; d tr – double treble: yarn round hook twice, insert hook, yarn round hook, pull through loop (4 loops on hook), [yarn round hook, pull it through 2 loops] 3 times; in – inches;

# MAKING THE COVER

## Lace

To make the lace edging, ** make 8 **chain** 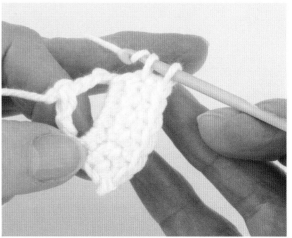,

ROW 3 1 ch, 1 dc in each of next 5 dc,

1 **double treble** (see abbreviations on page 100) in first ch, turn.

ROW 1 1 ch,

2 dc in ch, turn.

ROW 4 1 ch, 1 dc in each of next 6 dc, 1 dc in ch, do not turn.

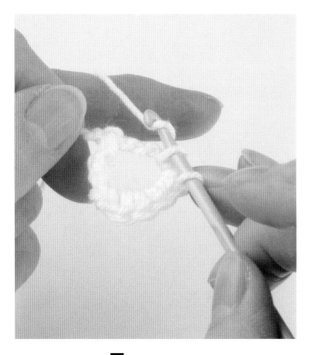

6 **double crochet** 10 around half of 8 ch, turn.

ROW 2 1 ch, 1 dc in each of next 5 dc, 1 dc in ch, turn.

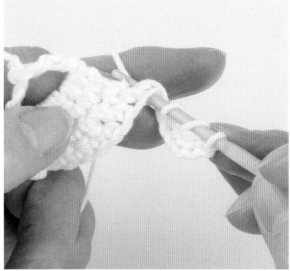

Repeat from ** until 20 patterns have been completed, or until lace is required length (check width of coat hanger and add a little to accommodate garment).

Do not fasten off.

## Edging

When working in row ends insert hook under two strands of yarn as usual: 1 ch,

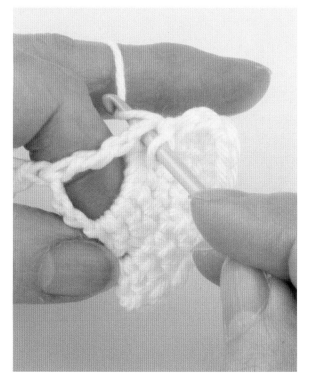

1 dc in each of next 3 dc row ends, * 4 dc around d tr, 1 dc in each of next 4 dc row ends; repeat from *, ending 3 dc around d tr, 1 dc in first ch.
**Fasten off 21 .**

## Finishing

Pin out lace to required length, keeping top edge straight and pinning the points to shape. Press, using steam or a damp cloth.

Make a paper pattern for the cover – the lower edge to fit the lace doubled, the top shaped by drawing around the coat hanger and adding a 2cm (¾ in) seam allowance around all edges. Cut out 2 fabric pieces. Right sides together, stitch these around sides and top, leaving an opening for the hook. Neaten this opening and seams. Turn through to the right side. Make a small hem along the lower edge and hand stitch the lace to this, joining the ends neatly at one side seam. Spray starch, if required.

# Bath Mat

Treat your toes to a firm white cotton bath mat with a textured star design.

The bobbles forming the star are called popcorns. Because a popcorn is a group of trebles gathered with a single stitch at the top it's very well defined and durable.

## You will need

3 x 100g balls Sirdar Pure Cotton DK
3.50mm hook

## Size

Approximately 41cm x 61cm (16½ in x 24½ in)

## Tension

18 tr and 10 rows to 10cm (4in) over tr with 3.50mm hook

## Abbreviations

ch – chain; cm – centimetres;  in – inches;
pc – popcorn: work 5 tr in next st, take out hook leaving loop, insert hook from front to back in top of first tr then into loop, yarn round hook, pull yarn through both loop and tr;  st(s) – stitch(es); tr – treble

# MAKING THE MAT

## Mat

Make 77 **chain** **6** .

**ROW 1** Miss 3 ch, * 1 **treble** **11** in next ch; repeat from * to end. 75 sts.

**ROW 2** 3 ch, * 1 tr in next tr; repeat from *, ending 1 tr in top ch of 3 ch.

Repeat row 2 16 times, making a total of 18 rows.

## Making a popcorn

To make a popcorn (abbreviation pc),

Take out the hook, leave the loop and insert the hook from front to back in the first tr of the group of 5.

first make 5 tr in the next stitch.

Insert the hook in the loop, yarn round hook and pull it through both loop and tr to complete the popcorn.

**ROW 19** (right side)  3 ch, [1 tr in next tr] 36 times, 1 popcorn (see illustrations, left) in next tr, [1 tr in next tr] 36 times, 1 tr in top ch of 3 ch.

**ROW 20**  (On wrong-side rows a treble and a popcorn are both now referred to as a st)  3 ch, * 1 tr in next st; repeat from *, ending 1 tr in top ch of 3 ch.

**ROW 21**  3 ch, [1 tr in next tr] 34 times, 1 pc in next tr, 1 tr in each of next 3 tr,

**ROW 22** and wrong-side rows  As row 20.

**ROW 23**  3 ch, [1 tr in next tr] 32 times, [1 pc in next tr, 1 tr in each of next 3 tr] twice, 1 pc in next tr, [1 tr in next tr] 32 times, 1 tr in top ch of 3 ch.

**ROW 25**  3 ch, [1 tr in next tr] 18 times, [1 pc in next tr, 1 tr in each of next 3 tr] 9 times, 1 pc in next tr, [1 tr in next tr] 18 times, 1 tr in top ch of 3 ch.

**ROW 27**  3 ch, [1 tr in next tr] 20 times, [1 pc in next tr, 1 tr in each of next 3 tr] 8 times, 1 pc in next tr, [1 tr in next tr] 20 times, 1 tr in top ch of 3 ch.

**ROW 29**  3 ch, [1 tr in next tr] 22 times, [1 pc in next tr, 1 tr in each of next 3 tr] 7 times, 1 pc in next tr, [1 tr in next tr] 22 times, 1 tr in top ch of 3 ch.

**ROW 31**  3 ch, [1 tr in next tr] 24 times, [1 pc in next tr, 1 tr in each of next 3 tr] 6 times, 1 pc in next tr, [1 tr in next tr] 24 times, 1 tr in top ch of 3 ch.

**ROW 33**  As row 29.

**ROW 35**  As row 27.

**ROW 37**  As row 25.

**ROW 39**  As row 23.

**ROW 41**  As row 21.

**ROW 43**  As row 19.

Now work 18 rows as row 20.

Total 61 rows.

**Fasten off 21 .**

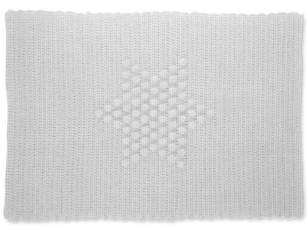

1 pc in next tr, [1 tr in next tr] 34 times, 1 tr in top ch of 3 ch.

# Baby Blanket

Wrap baby in a generous warm blanket that's chequered in two toning colours.

Patterning two colours together instead of separately is tricky at first, but with a little patience it becomes routine to change colour in mid stitch and to carry one yarn invisibly by working around it with the other.

## You will need

11 x 50g balls of Jaeger Baby Merino DK:
    5 balls lilac (A)
    6 balls pale lilac (B)
5.00mm hook
4.50mm hook

## Size

Approximately 77cm x 102cm (30½ in x 41in)

## Tension

17 sts and 9 rows to 10cm (4in) over pattern with 4.50mm hook

## Abbreviations

cc – colour change: with first colour, yarn round hook, insert hook in next st, yarn round hook and pull through to make 3 loops on hook, yarn round hook and pull it through the next 2 loops on hook, change to 2nd colour, yarn round hook, pull yarn through 2 remaining loops to complete tr; ch – chain; cm – centimetres; in – inches; ss – slip stitch; st(s) – stitch(es); tr – treble

# MAKING THE BLANKET

## Colour changing

Changing a colour halfway through making a stitch (abbreviation cc) gives a neater result than changing between stitches.

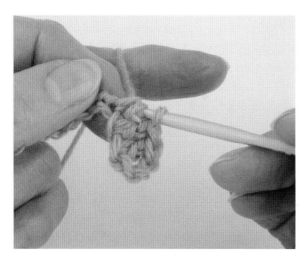

With first colour, yarn round hook, insert hook in next st, yarn round hook and pull through to make 3 loops on hook, yarn round hook and pull through the next 2 loops on the hook.

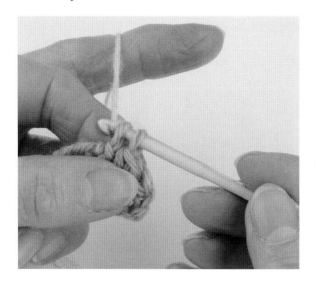

With second colour, yarn round hook, pull yarn through 2 remaining loops to complete a tr.

## Blanket

With 5.00mm hook and A, make 121 **chain** **6** .
Change to 4.50mm hook.
**ROW** 1(right side)  Miss 3 ch, 1 **treble** **11** in each of next 2 ch, **colour change** (see the instructions, left) in next ch, * with B,

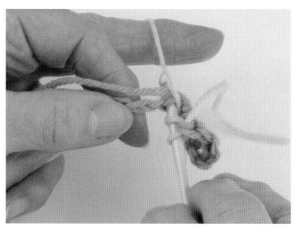

working each tr around A, 1 tr in each of next 2 ch, cc in next ch, with A, working each tr around B, 1 tr in each of next 2 ch, cc in next ch; rep from *, ending with A, but not working around B,

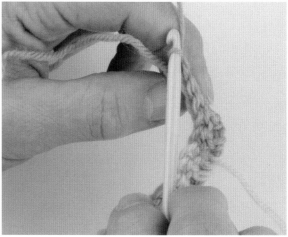

1 tr in each of next 4 ch.
119 sts.

**ROW 2** With A, 3 ch, 1 tr in each of next 2 tr, cc in next tr, * working around colour not in use as before, with B, 1 tr in each of next 2 tr, cc in next tr, with A, 1 tr in each of next 2 tr, cc in next tr; rep from *,

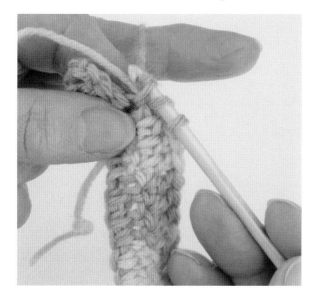

ending with A, working around B, 1 tr in each of next 3 tr, 1 tr in top ch of 3 ch. Continue to work around colour not in use when it needs to be carried to a new block of colour.

**ROW 3** With B, 3 ch, 1 tr in each of next 2 tr, cc in next tr, * with A, 1 tr in each of next 2 tr, cc in next tr, with B, 1 tr in each of next 2 tr, cc in next tr; rep from *, ending with B, 1 tr in each of next 3 tr, 1 tr in top ch of 3 ch.

**ROW 4** As row 3.

**ROW 5** With A, 3 ch, 1 tr in each of next 2 tr, cc in next tr, * with B, 1 tr in each of next 2 tr, cc in next tr, with A, 1 tr in each of next 2 tr, cc in next tr; rep from *, ending with A, 1 tr in each of next 3 tr, 1 tr in top ch of 3 ch.

Rep rows 2-5  20 times, then work row 2 again. 86 rows.

**Fasten off 21 .**

**Edging**

With right side facing, using 4.50mm hook and B:

**ROUND 1** **Join yarn 20** in top right hand corner, work (3 ch, 2 tr) in corner st, * 1 tr in each st to next corner, 3 tr in corner, 2 tr around each tr to next corner, * 3 tr in corner; rep from * to * , ending at first corner, **slip stitch 7** to top ch of 3 ch.

**ROUND 2** 3 ch, 3 tr in next st, * 1 tr in each st to next corner, 3 tr in 2nd of 3 tr; rep from *, ending ss to top ch of 3 ch.

**ROUND 3** 3 ch, 1 tr in next st, 3 tr in next st, * 1 tr in each st to next corner, 3 tr in 2nd of 3 tr; rep from * , ending ss to top ch of 3 ch.

**ROUND 4** With A and starting in one corner, (1 ch, 1 **double crochet 10** ) in corner st, * 1 dc in each st to next corner, 2 dc in corner st; rep from *, ending ss to 1 ch.

Fasten off.

**Darn in ends 24 .**

Press.

# Ruffled Scarf

Although it could be worn as a boa, this long scarf is designed to be coiled round the neck in flattering ruffles.

It grows quickly because the stitch is double treble with some chain. Lots of increases make the crochet curl and spiral.

## You will need

2 x 50g balls Debbie Bliss Cotton Cashmere in crimson
5.50mm hook

## Size

Approximately 125cm (50in) long

## Tension

5 sts and 2 rows to 5cm (2in) over d tr with 5.50mm hook

## Abbreviations

ch – chain; cm – centimetres; dc – double crochet; d tr – double treble: yarn round hook twice, insert hook, yarn round hook, pull through a loop to make 4 loops on hook, [yarn round hook, pull it through next 2 loops on hook] 3 times; in – inches

# MAKING THE SCARF

## Scarf

Make 160 **chain** `6`.

**ROW 1**  Miss 3 ch, * 1 **double treble** (see abbreviations on page 113) in next ch;

repeat from *, ending 2 d tr in last ch.

**ROW 2**  4 ch,

1 d tr in d tr below, * 2 d tr in next d tr; repeat from *, ending 2 d tr in top ch of 3 ch.

**ROW 3**  5 ch,

* 1 d tr in next d tr, 1 ch; repeat from *, ending 1 d tr in top ch of 4 ch.

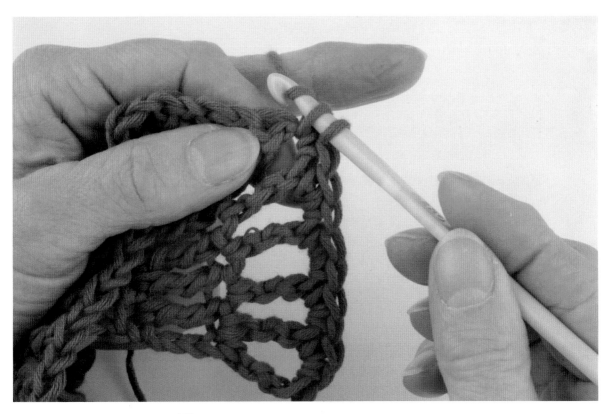

ROW 4  1 ch, * 2 **double crochet** 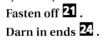 in next chain space; repeat from *, ending 1 dc in 4th of 5 ch.

**Fasten off** **21** .

**Darn in ends** **24** .

# Frilly Bag

An explosion of frills around the top is the main feature of this frivolous little handbag.

The frills are a good example of an interesting effect achieved with simple stitches. Three rounds of open mesh around the top of the bag (trebles and chain) are used as a base for closely-worked trebles, which then stand away from the bag as crisp frills.

## You will need

3 x 50g balls of Rowan Handknit Cotton
3.00mm hook
3.50mm hook

## Size

Approximately 19cm wide x 16cm high (7½in x 6in)

## Tension

18 tr and 10 rows to 10cm (4in) with 3.50mm hook

## Abbreviations

ch – chain; cm – centimetres; dc – double crochet;
in – inches; sp – space(s); ss – slip stitch; sts – stitches;
tr – treble

# MAKING THE BAG

## Sides

With 3.50mm hook, make 72 **chain** 6 and without twisting, join with **slip stitch** 7 to form a **ring** 9. Work in **rounds** 14 with right side facing:

**ROUND 1** 3 ch, 1 **treble** 11 in each ch to end, without twisting ss to top ch of 3 ch. 72 sts.

**ROUND 2** 3 ch, 1 tr in each tr to end, ss to top ch of 3 ch. Repeat round 2 9 times.

**ROUND 12** 5 ch,

[miss 2 tr, 1 tr in next tr, 2 ch] 22 times, ss to 3rd of 5 ch. 24 sp.

**ROUND 13** 5 ch, [1 tr in next tr, 2 ch] 22 times, ss to 3rd of 5 ch.

**ROUND 14** As round 13.

**Fasten off** 21.

## Frill

With 3.00mm hook:

**ROUND 1** Folding back rounds 12–14 to be out of the way, **join yarn** 20 to first tr of round 11, work 3 ch, 1 tr in this tr and

2 tr in next tr, * turn work 45 degrees, fold along first

tr of round 12 and work 4 tr around the post of this tr, * turn, fold and work 4 tr around 2 ch, turn, fold and work

4 tr around post of next tr, turn, fold and work

2 tr in each of next 2 tr of round 11, turn, fold and work

4 tr around post of next tr; repeat from *, ending 4 tr around 2 ch, 4 tr around first 3 ch of 5 ch, ss to top ch of 3 ch.
Fasten off.

**ROUND 2** In first sp of round 12 join yarn and work 3 ch, 3 tr around 2 ch, turn and fold, 4 tr around post of first tr of round 13, * turn and fold, 4 tr around 2 ch, turn and fold, 4 tr around post of next tr, turn and fold, 4 tr around 2 ch, turn and fold, 4 tr around post of next tr; repeat from *, ending 4 tr in 2 ch, 4 tr in first 3 ch of 5 ch, ss to top ch of 3 ch.
Fasten off.

**ROUND 3** Starting in first sp of round 13, work as round 2.
Fasten off.

**ROUND 4** In first sp of round 14 join yarn and work 1 ch, 2 **double crochet** 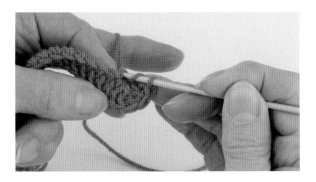 around 2 ch, * 3 ch, 3 dc around next 2 ch; repeat from *, ending 3 ch, ss to 1 ch.
Fasten off.

## Base

With 3.50mm hook, make 30 ch.
**ROUND 1** Miss 3 ch, 1 tr in each of next 26 ch,

5 tr in last ch, without turning work over, work 1 tr in each remaining single strand of 26 ch, 4 tr in first of 3 ch, ss to top ch of 3 ch.  62 sts
**ROUND 2** 3 ch, 1 tr in each of next 26 tr, 2 tr in each of next 5 tr, 1 tr in each of next 26 tr, 2 tr in each of next 4 tr, 1 tr in ss, ss to top ch of 3 ch.  72 sts
Fasten off.

## Handles

(make 2)
With 3.50mm hook, make 100 ch.
Miss 1 ch, * ss in next ch; repeat from * to end, 1 ch, ss in the remaining single strand of each of 99 ch.
Fasten off, leaving an end long enough to sew with.

## Finishing

Flatten sides so that join forms side seam, then match side seam to centre 10 tr of base. Place base and sides wrong sides together and using a 3.00mm hook, **join with double crochet**  **,** inserting hook in a single strand of a foundation ch of sides and an edge stitch of base each time. On each side, pull a handle through an open space in last row of frills, join the ends and secure the join to the bag.

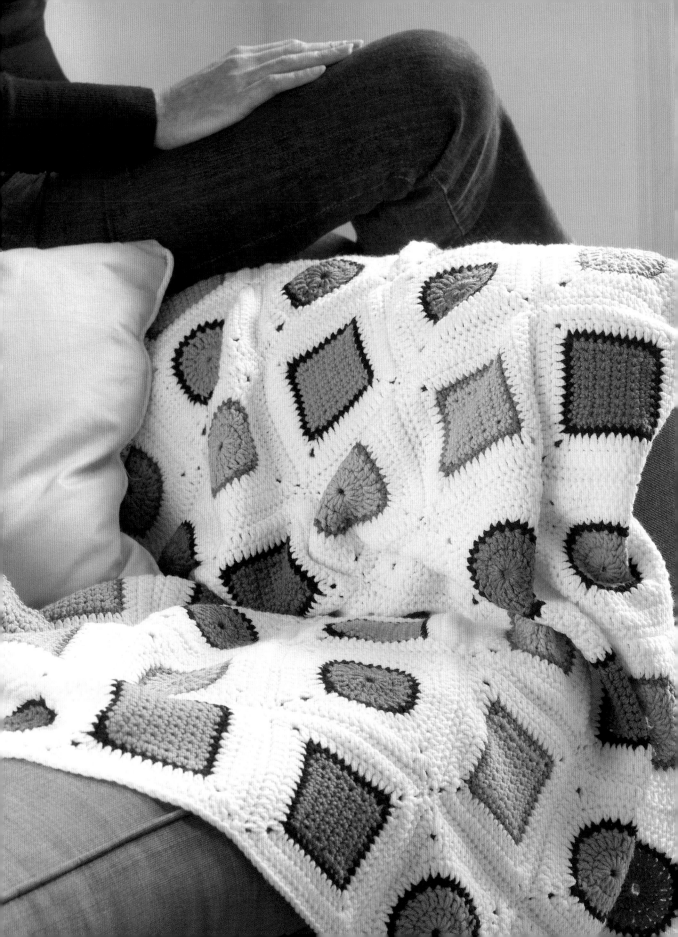

# Retro Throw

There's something deliberately reminiscent of the 1960's in this geometric and almost monochromatic woollen throw.

The motif with the circular centre is constructed in rounds and then its corners are squared up. The centre of the square motif is worked in rows for a well-defined shape and then it is completed in rounds so that all the edges match.

## You will need

15 x 50g balls of Jaeger Extra Fine Merino DK
> 2 balls charcoal (A or B)
> 2 balls flannel (A)
> 1 ball black (B)
> 1 ball lime (A)
> 9 balls white (C)

4.50mm hook

## Size

Approximately 73cm x 109cm (29in x 44in)

## Tension

Each square measures approximately 13cm (5in) with a 4.50mm hook

## Abbreviations

ch – chain; ch sp – chain space; cm – centimetres; dc – double crochet; in – inches; ss – slip stitch; st(s) – stitch(es); tr – treble

# MAKING THE THROW

## Square motif

(make 25)

With A, make 10 **chain** .

ROW 1 Miss 2 ch, 1 **double crochet** [10] in each of next 8 ch. 9 sts.

ROW 2 1 ch, 1 dc in each of next 7 dc, 1 dc in top ch of 2 ch.

ROW 3 1 ch, 1 dc in each of next 7 dc, 1 dc in ch.

Repeat row 3 6 times, making a total of 9 rows. Do not fasten off and do not turn work over.

Now work in **rounds** [14] with right side facing:

ROUND 1 Around the square work: 3 ch, 1 dc in each of 8 row ends, (1 dc, 2 ch, 1 dc) in last row end, 1 dc over each of 7 sts of 1st row, (1 dc, 1 ch, 1 dc) in last st of row, 1 dc in each of 7 row ends, (1 dc, 1 ch, 1 dc) in last row end,

1 dc in each of 7 sts of last row, join with **slip stitch** [7] to first of 3 ch.

**Fasten off** [21] A.

ROUND 2 With B, pull through a loop in one corner ch sp to **join yarn** [20] , 3 ch, 1 dc in ch sp, [1 dc in each of next 9 dc,

(1 dc, 2 ch, 1 dc) in corner ch sp] 3 times, 1 dc in each of next 8 dc, 1 dc in ss, ss to first of 3 ch. 44 sts plus corner ch.

Fasten off B.

**ROUND 3** With C, pull through a loop in one corner ch sp, 5 ch, 1 **treble**  in ch sp, [1 tr in each of next 11 dc, (1 tr, 2 ch, 1 tr) in corner ch sp] 3 times,

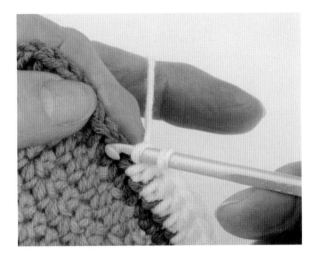

1 tr in each of next 10 dc, 1 dc in ss, ss to 3rd of 5 ch, ss in 5-ch sp. 52 sts plus corner ch.

**ROUND 4** 3 ch, (1 tr, 2 ch, 2 tr) in 5-ch sp,

[1 tr in each of next 13 tr, (2 tr, 2 ch, 2 tr) in corner ch sp] 3 times, 1 tr in each of next 12 tr, 1 tr in ss, ss to top ch of 3 ch. 68 sts plus corner ch.
Fasten off.

## Round motif

(make 29)

With A, make 5 **chain** [6], ss into first ch to make a **chain ring** [9].

**ROUND 1** 3 ch, 15 tr in ring, ss to top ch of 3 ch. 16 sts.

**ROUND 2** 3 ch, [2 tr in next tr, 1 tr in next tr] 7 times, 2 tr in next tr, ss to top ch of 3 ch. 24 sts.
Fasten off A.

**ROUND 3** With B, pull through a loop in next st to **join yarn** [20], 1 ch, [2 dc in next tr,

1 dc in next tr] 11 times, 2 dc in next tr, ss to 1 ch. 36 sts.
Fasten off B.

123

**ROUND 4** With C, pull through a loop in next st, 3 ch, 1 tr in next dc, [2 tr in next dc, 1 tr in each of next 2 dc] 11 times, 2 tr in next dc,

ss to top ch of 3 ch. 48 sts.

**ROUND 5** 5 ch, 1 tr in base of 1st ch, 1 tr in next tr, [1 dc in each of next 9 tr, 1 tr in next tr, (1 tr, 2 ch, 1 tr) in next tr, 1 tr in next tr] 3 times,

1 dc in each of next 9 tr, 1 tr in next tr, ss to 3rd ch of 5 ch, ss in 5-ch sp. 52 sts plus corner ch.

**ROUND 6** 3 ch, (1 tr, 2 ch, 2 tr) in 5-ch sp, [1 tr in each of next 13 sts, (2 tr, 2 ch, 2 tr) in corner ch sp] 3 times,

1 tr in each of next 12 sts, 1 tr in first ss of previous round, ss to top ch of 3 ch. 68 sts plus corner ch. Fasten off.

Make a total of 54 motifs: 8 square motifs with charcoal as A and black as B, 10 with flannel as A and charcoal as B, 7 with lime as A and black as B; 10 round motifs with charcoal as A and black as B, 11 with flannel as A and charcoal as B, 8 with lime as A and black as B. All squares have white as C.

## Finishing

Damp press the squares to shape. Arrange the squares in a rectangle of 6 across and 9 down, with all final ends lying in the same direction. With right sides together and using C, take pairs of squares and **join with double crochet 22**, inserting the hook under the inner strand of each edge stitch until all the shorter rows have been joined, then join all the longer rows.

### Edging

With right side facing and using C, starting with 1 ch in any square, * work 1 dc in each edge st,

1 tr in each seam and 3 dc in each corner, ending ss in 1 ch.
Fasten off.

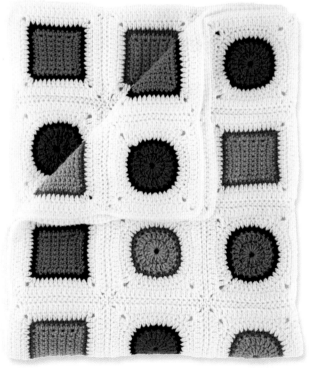

# Yarn Information

The following information will help you to make a substitution if the yarn used in a project is not available. Be sure to check the pattern, look at the ball bands, and compare the new yarn with the information below to be sure the substitution is an appropriate one. Remember that the people who work in the store should be both knowledgeable and eager to help.

**Debbie Bliss Cathay**
Double-knitting-weight cotton, viscose, and silk yarn
50% Cotton/35% Viscose/15% Silk
Approximately 100m (108yds) per 50g (1¾oz) ball

**Debbie Bliss Cotton Cashmere**
Double-knitting-weight cotton and cashmere
85% cotton/15% cashmere
Approximately 95m (103yds) per 50g (1¾oz) ball

**Debbie Bliss Cotton DK**
Double-knitting-weight cotton
100% cotton
Approximately 84m (91yds) per 50g (1¾oz) ball

**Debbie Bliss Merino DK**
Double-knitting-weight wool
100% merino wool
Approximately 110m (120yds) per 50g (1¾oz) ball

**Jaeger Aqua**
Double-knitting-weight cotton
100% mercerized cotton
Approximately 106m (116yds) per 50g (1¾oz) ball

**Jaeger Baby Merino DK**
Double-knitting-weight wool
100% merino wool
Approximately 120m (130yds) per 50g (1¾oz) ball

**Jaeger Extra Fine Merino DK**
Double-knitting-weight wool
100% extra-fine merino wool
Approximately 125m (137yds) per 50g (1¾oz) ball

**Jaeger Matchmaker DK**
Double-knitting-weight wool
100% merino wool
Approximately 120m (130yds) per 50g (1¾oz) ball

**Jaeger Matchmaker Merino Aran**
Aran-weight merino wool
100% merino wool
Approximately 82m (90yds) per 50g (1¾oz) ball

**Rowan 4-ply Soft**
4-ply wool yarn
100% merino wool
Approximately 175m (190yds) per 50g (1¾oz) ball

**Rowan Cotton Glace**
Lightweight cotton yarn
100% cotton
Approximately 115m (125yds) per 50g (1¾oz) ball

**Rowan Denim**
Medium-weight cotton yarn
100% cotton
Approximately 93m (101yds) per 50g (1¾oz) ball

**Rowan Handknit Cotton**
Medium-weight cotton yarn
100% cotton
Approximately 85m (92yds) per 50g (1¾oz) ball

**Rowan Wool Cotton**
Double-knitting-weight wool and cotton
50% merino wool/50% cotton
Approximately 113m (123yds) per 50g (1¾oz) ball

**Sirdar Pure Cotton DK**
Double-knitting-weight cotton
100% cotton
Approximately 169m (184yds) per 100g (3½oz) ball

# Yarn Suppliers

**ROWAN & JAEGER YARNS**

**UK**
Rowan
Green Lane Mill
Holmfirth
West Yorkshire HD9 2DX
Tel: +44 (0)1484 681881
www.knitrowan.com

**USA**
Westminster Fibers Inc.
4 Townsend West
Suite 8
Nashua, NH 03063
Tel: +1 603 886 5041
E-mail: rowan@westminsterfibers.com

**Canada**
Diamond Yarn
9697 St Laurent
Montreal
Quebec H3L 2N1
Tel: +1 514 388 6188

**Australia**
Australian Country Spinners
314 Albert Street
Brunswick,
Victoria 3056
Tel +61 (0)3 9380 3888

**France**
Elle Tricote
8 Rue du Coq
(Petit France)
67000 Strasbourg
Tel: +33 (0)388 230313
www.elletricote.com.fr

**Germany**
Woll Boutique
Wandsbeker Chaussee 315
Hamburg
Tel: +49 (0)40 2007620
E-mail: service@wollboutique.de
www.wollboutique.de

**Belgium**
Art el Fil
Rue du Bailli 25
Brussels
Tel: +32 (0)2 647 6451

**Sweden**
Rowan at Wincent
Norrtullsgatan 65
113 45 Stockholm
Tel +46 8 33 70 60
E-mail: wincent@chelio.se
www.wincent.nu

**Denmark**
Wilferts
Gammel Kongevej 102
1850 Frederiksberg
Tel: +33 22 54 90
E-mail wilfert@webspeed.dk
www.wilferts.dk

**Norway**
Tjorven
Valkyriegt 17
Oslo
Tel: +47 22 69 33 60

**South Africa**
Arthur Bales Ltd
62 4th Avenue
Linden
Te: +27 118 882 401
E-mail: arthurb@new.co.za

**Japan**
Ebisu Mitsukoshi 2F
4-20-7 Ebisu Shibuyaku
Tokyo
Tel (0) 3 54231602
www.rowan-jaeger.com

**DEBBIE BLISS YARNS**

**UK**
Designer Yarns Limited
Units 8-10 Newbridge Industrial Estate
Pitt Street
Keighley
West Yorkshire BD21 4PQ
Tel +44 (0)1535 664222
www.designeryarns.uk.com

**USA**
Knitting Fever Inc
315 Bayview Avenue
Amityville
New York 11702
Tel: +1 516 546 3600
E-mail: admin@knittingfever.com
www.knittingfever.com

**Canada**
Diamond Yarns Ltd
155 Martin Ross Avenue
Unit 3,
Toronto
Ontario M3J 2L9
Tel +1 416 736 6111

**Australia**
Sunspun
185 Canterbury Road
Canterbury
VIC 3126
Tel: +61 (0)3 9830 1609
E-mail: shop@sunspun.com.au

Jo Sharp Pty Ltd
PO Box 1018
Freemantle
WA 6959
Tel: +61 (0)8 9430 9699
E-mail: yarn@josharp.com.au

**France**
Elle Tricote
8 Rue du Coq
(Petit France)
67000 Strasbourg
Tel: +33 (0)388 230313
www.elletricote.com.fr

**Germany/Austria/Switzerland**
Designer Yarns
Handelsagentur
Klaus Koch
Mauritius Str. 130
50226 Frechen
Tel: +49 2234 205453
www.designeryarns.de

**Belgium/Holland**
Pavan
Meerlaanstraat 73
Oostrezele 9860
Tel +32 9221 8594
E-mail: pavan@pandora.be

**Sweden**
Hamilton Design
Langgatan 20
SE-64730
Mariefred
Tel +46 (0) 159 12006
www.hamiltondesign.biz

**Denmark**
Strikkeboden
Krystalgade 16
1172 Copenhagen K
Tel: +45 4583 0127
E-mail: jens.toersleff@get2net.dk

**Japan**
Eisaku Noro & Co Ltd
55 Shimoda Ohibino Azaichou
Ichinomita Aichi
4910105
Te: +81 52 203 5100
www.eisakunoro.com

SIRDAR YARNS
**UK**
Sirdar Spinning Limited
Flanshaw Lane
Alverthorpe
Wakefield
West Yorkshire WF2 9ND

**USA**
Knitting Fever Inc
315 Bayview Avenue
Amityville
New York 11702
Tel: +1 516 546 3600
E-mail: admin@knittingfever.com
www.knittingfever.com

**Canada**
Diamond Yarn
9697 St Laurent
Suite 101
Montreal
Quebec H3L 2N1
Tel: + 1 514 388 6188
E-mail: diamond@diamondyarn.com
www.diamondyarn.com

Diamond Yarn
155 Martin Ross
Unit 3
Toronto
Ontario M3J 2L9
Tel: + 1 416 736 6111
E-mail:
diamond@diamondyarn.com
www.diamondyarn.com

**Australia**
Creative Images
PO Box 106
Hastings
Victoria 3915
Australia
Tel: + 61 (0)3 5979 1555
E-mail:
creative@peninsula.starway.net.au

**Germany**
Hansa Contec GmbH
Schpenstehl 22
D - 20095 Hamburg
Tel: + 49 (0)40 333 95622
E-mail: office@hansacontec.de

**The Netherlands**
Breiweb
Hoofdstraat 44
7751 GD DALEN (Dr)
Tel: + 31 (0) 524-551597
E-mail: info@breiweb.nl
www.breiweb.nl

**Sweden**
Almedahls AB
Stationsvagen 2
S-516 80 Dalsjofors
Tel: + 46 334 80100
E-mail:   info@almedhals.se
www.almedhals.se

**Norway**
AS Knappehuset
Postboks 100
Ulset
5873 Bergen
Tel: + 47 5553 9300
E-mail:   post@knappehuset.no
www.knappehuset.no

**South Africa**
Saprotex International (Pty)
PO Box 1293
East London
5200
Tel: + 27 43 763 1551
E-mail: tbarratt@bertrand.co.za
www.knit1.net

# Acknowledgements

Thanks to Hilary Underwood, who
helped with the crochet, and to Susan
Horan, who checked the instructions.